Microwave VEGETARIAN

BRAMLEY BOOKS

Compiled and Edited by Judith Ferguson
Designed by Philip Clucas
Photography by Peter Barry
Produced by Ted Smart,
David Gibbon and Gerald Hughes

CLB 1741
This edition published 1986 by Bramley Books, Godalming, Surrey.
© 1986 Illustrations and text: Colour Library Books Ltd.,
   Guildford, Surrey.
Printed and bound in Barcelona, Spain.
All rights reserved.
ISBN 0 86283 492 9

CONTENTS

GENERAL INTRODUCTION

People are usually of two minds about microwave ovens. Experienced cooks are sceptical. Inexperienced cooks are mystified. Most people who don't own one think a microwave oven is an expensive luxury. Those of us who have one, though, would find it difficult to give it up. Great advances have been made in the design and capabilities of microwave ovens since the demand for them first began in the Sixties. With so many kinds of ovens available, both beginners and advanced cooks can find one that best suits their particular needs.

How Microwave Ovens Work

Microwave ovens, whatever the make or model, do have certain things in common. The energy that makes fast cooking possible is comprised of electromagnetic waves converted from electricity. Microwaves are a type of high frequency radio wave. The waves are of short length, hence the name microwave.

Inside the oven is a magnetron, which converts ordinary electricity into microwaves. A wave guide channels the microwaves into the oven cavity, and a stirrer fan circulates them evenly. Microwaves are attracted to the particles of moisture that form part of any food. As the microwaves are absorbed, to a depth of about 4-5cm/1^{1}/$_{2}$-2 inches, they cause the water molecules in the food to vibrate, about 2000 million times a second. This generates the heat that cooks the food. The heat reaches the centre of the food by conduction, just as in ordinary cooking. However, this is accomplished much faster than in conventional cooking because no heat is generated until

the waves are absorbed by the food. All the energy is concentrated on cooking the food and not on heating the oven itself or the baking dishes. Standing time is often necessary to allow the food to continue cooking after it is removed from the oven.

Most microwave ovens have an ON indicator light and a timer control. Some timer controls look like minute timers, while others are calibrated in seconds up to 50 seconds and minutes up to 30 minutes. This can vary slightly; some models have a 10 minute interval setting. Some ovens have a separate ON-OFF switch, while others switch on with the timer or power setting. Almost all have a bell or buzzer to signal the end of cooking time.

Microwave Oven Features

At this point, things really begin to diversify. Different terms are used for the same power setting depending on what brand of oven you buy. Some ovens have a wider range of different settings as well. Chart No. 1 on power settings reconciles most of the popular terms.

Some ovens come equipped with a temperature probe which allows you to cook food according to its internal temperature instead of by time. It is most useful for roasting large cuts of meat. The probe needle is inserted into the thickest part of the food and the correct temperature set on the attached control. When that internal temperature is reached, the oven automatically turns off, or switches to a low setting to keep the

food warm. Special microwave thermometers are also available to test internal temperature and can be used inside the oven. Conventional thermometers must never be used inside a microwave oven, but can be used outside.

A cooking guide is a feature on some ovens, either integrated into the control panel or on the top or side of the oven housing. It is really a summary of the information found in the instruction and recipe booklet that accompanies every oven. However, it does act as a quick reference and so can be a time saver.

Turntables eliminate the need for rotating baking dishes during cooking, although when using a square or loaf dish you may need to change its position from time to time anyway. Turntables are usually glass or ceramic and can be removed for easy cleaning. Of all the special features available, turntables are one of the most useful.

Certain ovens have one or more shelves so that several dishes can be accommodated at once. Microwave energy is higher at the top of the oven than on the floor and the more you cook at once the longer it all takes. However, these ovens accommodate larger baking dishes than those with turntables.

If you do a lot of entertaining, then an oven with a keep warm setting is a good choice. These ovens have a very low

CHART 1 Power Setting Comparison Chart

	Other Terms and Wattages	Uses
Low	ONE or TWO, KEEP WARM, 25%, SIMMER, DEFROST. 75-300 watts.	Keeping food warm. Softening butter, cream cheese and chocolate. Heating liquid to dissolve yeast. Gentle cooking.
Medium	THREE or FOUR, 50%, STEW, BRAISE, ROAST, REHEAT, MEDIUM-LOW, FIVE, 40%, MEDIUM-HIGH, SIX, 60-75%. 400-500 watts.	Cooking hollandaise sauces. Baking cakes and custards.
High	SEVEN, FULL, ROAST, BAKE, NORMAL, 100%.	Quick cooking. vegetables, biscuits/cookies, pasta, rice, breads, pastry, desserts.

power setting that can keep food warm without further cooking for up to one hour. If you want to programme your oven like a computer, choose one with a memory control that can switch settings automatically during the cooking cycle.

Browning elements are now available built into microwave ovens. They look and operate much the same as conventional electric grills. If you already have a grill, you probably don't need a browning element. Some of the most recent ovens allow the browning element to be used at the same time as the microwave setting, which is a plus.

Combination ovens seem to be the answer to the problem of browning in a microwave oven. While the power settings go by different names in different models, generally there is a setting for microwave cooking alone, a convection setting with conventional electric heat and a setting which combines the two for almost the speed of microwave cooking with the browning ability of convection heat. However, the wattage is usually lower than in standard microwave ovens, and so cooking time will be slightly longer.

You can have your microwave oven built into the same unit as your conventional oven. Microwave ovens are best situated at eye level. In fact, there are now units available with gas or electric cooktops and a microwave oven underneath where the conventional oven used to be.

Safety and Cleaning

One of the questions most commonly asked is "Are microwave ovens safe to use?" They are safe because they have safety features built into them and they go through rigorous tests by their manufacturers and by independent agencies.

If you look at a number of microwave ovens you will see that the majority of them are lined with metal, and metal will not allow microwaves to pass through. The doors have special seals to keep the microwaves inside the oven and have cut-out devices to cut off microwave energy immediately the door is opened. There are no pans to upset, no open flames or hot elements and the interior of the oven stays cool enough to touch. Although microwave ovens don't heat baking dishes, the heat generated by the cooking food does, so it is a good idea to use oven gloves or pot holders to remove dishes from the oven. It is wise periodically to check the door of your oven to make sure it has not been bent. Check latches and hinges, too, to make sure they are in good working order. Don't use baking dishes that are too large to allow the turntable to rotate freely; this can cause the motor to over-heat or cause dents in the oven sides and door, lowering efficiency and affecting safety of operation.

Microwave ovens are cleaner and more hygienic to cook with than conventional gas and electric ovens. Foods do not spatter as much and spills do not burn, so clean-up is faster. The turntables and shelves can be removed for easier cleaning. Use non-abrasive cleansers and scrubbers, and be sure to wipe up any residue so that it does not build up around the door seals. Faster cooking times and lower electricity consumption combine to make microwave ovens cheaper to run, especially for cooking small amounts of food, than conventional ovens.

Once you have chosen your oven and understand what makes it work, the fun of cooking begins. There are some basic rules to remember, however, as with conventional cooking, but most of them are common sense.

Quantity

Food quantities affect cooking times. For example, one baked potato will take about 3-4 minutes, two will take about 6-7 minutes, four will take 10-11 minutes. Generally, if you double the quantity of a recipe, you need to increase the cooking time by about half as much again.

Size

The smaller a piece of food the quicker it will cook. Pieces of food of the same kind and size will cook at the same rate. Add smaller or faster-cooking foods further along in the cooking time, such as mushrooms to a stew. If you have a choice of cooking heights, put food that is larger and can take more heat above food that is smaller and more delicate.

Covering

Most foods will cook, reheat or defrost better when covered. Use special covers that come with your cookware or simple cover with cling film. This covering must be pierced to release steam, otherwise it can balloon and possibly burst.

Equipment and Cookware

The number of different baking dishes and the range of equipment for microwave cooking is vast. There are so many highly specialised dishes for specific needs that to list them all would take up almost the whole of this book!

Explore cookware departments and find your own favourites. Follow your oven instruction booklet carefully since it will give you good advice on which cookware is best for your particular oven. Some dishes, lightweight plastics and even some hard plastics can't be used on combination settings. The temperature is too high and the dishes will melt or break. Most metal cookware can be used successfully in combination ovens, following the manufacturers guidelines. I have had less than satisfactory results with certain aluminium pans in my combination oven, so experimentation is essential. Paper bags can catch fire on High settings, and I have had the same experience with silicone-coated paper, although its use is often recommended. Microwave energy penetrates round shapes particularly efficiently, so round dishes and ring moulds work very well. The turntable can also be cooked on directly for such

CHART 2 Cooking Vegetables

Type	Quantity	Water	Mins. on High	Mins. Stdg. Time
Artichokes	4	430ml/¾pt/1½ cups	10-20	5
Asparagus	450g/1lb	140ml/¼pt/½ cup	9-12	5
Aubergine/ Eggplant	2 med.	30ml/2 tbsps	7-10	5
Beans	450g/1lb	140ml/¼pt/½ cup		
Green, French			8	3
Broad/Lima			10	3
Beetroot/Beets Whole	2	60ml/2 fl oz/¼ cup	4-5	3
Broccoli	450g/1lb	140ml/¼ pt/½ cup	4-5	3
Brussels Sprouts	450g/1lb	60ml/2 fl oz/¼ cup	8-10	3-5
Cabbage	450g/1lb	140ml/¼ pint/½ cup		
Shredded			7-9	3
Quartered			9-12	5
Carrots	225g/8oz	140ml/¼ pint/½ cup		
Whole			10	6
Sliced			7	5
Cauliflower	450g/1lb			
Whole		280ml/½ pint/1 cup	11	3
Florets		140ml/¼ pint/½ cup	7	3
Chicory	4	60ml/2 fl oz/¼ cup (water or stock)	5	3
Corn-on-the-Cob	2 ears	60ml/2 fl oz/¼ cup	6	3
Courgettes/ Zucchini	450g/1lb	60ml/2 fl oz/¼ cup	5	3
Fennel	1 bulb	280ml/½ pint/1 cup boiling water		
Sliced			2-8	3
Quartered			10-12	3
Leeks, sliced	450g/1lb	140ml/¼ pint/½ cup	7-10	3
Mushrooms	225g/8oz	30ml/2 tbsps	2	3
Okra	225g/8oz	60ml/2 fl oz/¼ cup	4	3
Onions, small	225g/8oz	30ml/1 fl oz/2 tbsps	7-8	3
Sliced	2	60ml/2 fl oz/¼ cup	10	3
Parsnips	225g/8oz	140ml/¼ pint/½ cup	8-10	3
Peas, shelled	450g/1lb	140ml/¼ pint/½ cup	10-15	5
Peapods/ Mangetout	225g/8oz	140ml/¼ pint/½ cup	3	3
Peppers	2 sliced	60ml/2 fl oz/¼ cup	3	3
Potatoes				
New	450g/1lb	140ml/¼ pint/½ cup	10-12	5
Baked	2		9-12	10
Boiled	450g/1lb	140ml/¼ pint/½ cup	6-7	5
Spinach	225g/8oz		4-5	3
Turnips	225g/8oz	60ml/2 fl oz/¼ cup	12	3

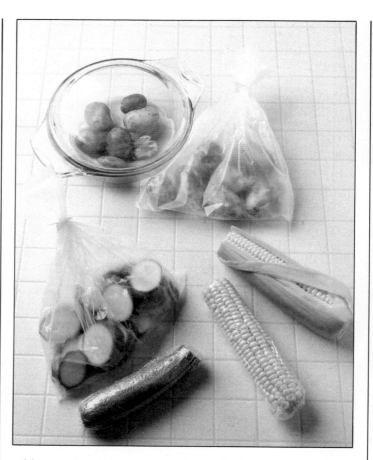

foods as scones or meringues or used for reheating foods like bread or coffee cakes.

Cooking Vegetables

Microwave cooking is ideal for vegetables. Very little water is needed, so they keep their colour and nutrients. They are best cooked loosely covered, and whole vegetables like corn-on-the-cob, aubergines, artichokes and chicory can be completely wrapped in cling film and cooked without any water. Cooking bags are another alternative.

Break broccoli into even-sized pieces and, if cooking a large quantity, be sure to put the flower ends in toward the centre of the dish. Trim down the tough ends of asparagus and peel the ends of the stalks. This will help the stalks cook quickly before the tips are overcooked. Some vegetables, like cucumbers, spring onions and button onions cook very well in butter or margarine alone, if well covered. Chart No. 2 lists suggested cooking times.

Cooking Fruit

Poach, bake and preserve fruit with ease in a microwave oven. Sterilise jars for preserving by adding a little water and heating on High for about 2-3 minutes and then draining. Metal lids and

rubbers seals are best sterilised outside the microwave oven. Paraffin wax for sealing jars cannot be melted in a microwave oven. The great advantages of microwave preserving are that jams and jellies can be made in small amounts and the job is much less messy and time-consuming. Whole preserved fruits and pickled vegetables can't be heated long enough to kill bacteria, so they must be kept refrigerated after bottling.

Cooking Rice, Pasta, Grains and Pulses

Rice and pasta need nearly as much cooking by microwave methods as by conventional ones. However, both pasta and rice cook without sticking together and without the chance of overcooking. This is because most of the actual cooking is accomplished during standing time. All kinds of rice and shapes of pasta benefit from being put into hot water with a pinch of salt and 5ml/1 tsp oil in a deep bowl. There is no need to cover the bowl during cooking, but, during standing time, a covering of some sort will help retain heat. Ease long spaghetti into the bowl gradually as it softens. Drain rice and pasta and rinse under hot water to remove starch. Both pasta and rice can be reheated in a microwave oven without loss of texture. Fresh pasta doesn't seem to take to the microwave oven successfully.

There is a great time saving with dried peas, beans and lentils — pulses. Cover them with water in a large bowl and heat

on a High setting to bring to the boil, which takes about 10 minutes. Allow the pulses to boil for about 2 minutes and then leave to stand for one hour. This cuts out overnight soaking. The pulses will cook in about 45 minutes to one hour depending on what variety is used. This is about half the conventional cooking time. Make sure pulses are cooked completely; it can be dangerous to eat them undercooked. Refer to Chart No. 3 for cooking times.

Cooking Eggs and Cheese

When poaching eggs, always pierce the yolks with a skewer or fork to prevent them from bursting. Use individual ramekins or patty pans with a spoonful of water in each. Alternatively, bring water to the boil in a large dish and add a pinch of salt and 5ml/l tsp vinegar to help set the egg whites. Slip the eggs in one at a time. Cook just until the whites are set. To stop the cooking and to keep the eggs from drying out, keep them in a bowl of cold water. For frying eggs, choose a browning dish, and for scrambling use a deep bowl or glass measuring jug. Always remove scrambled eggs from the oven while they are still very

soft. Stir during standing time to finish cooking. Hollandaise sause is easy to make. Choose the same kind of container as for scrambled eggs and have a bowl of iced water ready. Use a medium setting and cook the sauce at short intervals, whisking vigorously in between times. Put the sauce bowl into the iced water at the first sign of curdling or briefly when it has thickened, to stop the cooking process.

CHART 3 Cooking Rice, Pasta, Grains and Pulses

Type	Quantity	Water	Mins. on High	Mins. Stdg. Time
Brown Rice	120g/4oz/ 1 cup	570ml/1 pint/ 2 cups	20	5
White Rice (long grain)	120g/4oz/ 1 cup	570ml/1 pint/ 2 cups	10-12	5
Quick Cooking Rice	120g/4oz/ 1 cup	430ml/¾ pint/ 1½ cups	6	5
Macaroni	225g/8oz/ 3 cups	1 litre/1¾ pints/ 3½ cups	6	10
Quick Cooking Macaroni	225g/8oz/ 3 cups	1 litre/1¾ pints/ 3½ cups	3	10
Spaghetti	225g/8oz	1 litre/1¾ pints/ 3½ cups	6-10	10
Tagliatelle/Fettucine	225g/8oz	1 litre/1¾ pints/ 3½ cups	5-9	10
Pasta Shapes	225g/8oz/ 3 cups	1 litre/1¾ pints/ 3½ cups	6	10
Lasagne Ravioli Cannelloni	180g-225g/ 6oz-8oz	1 litre/1¾ pints/ 3½ cups	6	10
Barley	120g/4oz/ 1 cup	570ml/1 pint/ 2 cups	20	10
Bulgur (cracked wheat)	225g/8oz/ 2 cups	570ml/1 pint/ 2 cups boiling water	4	10
Dried Beans	180g/6oz/ 1 cup	1 litre/1¾ pints/ 3½ cups	55-60	10
Dried Peas	225g/8oz/ 3 cups	1 litre/1¾ pints/ 3½ cups	45-60	10
Lentils	225g/8oz/ 3 cups	1 litre/1¾ pints/ 3½ cups	20-25	15

NOTE: Add a pinch of salt and 5ml/1 tsp oil to grains and pasta

Cheese will get very stringy if it overcooks or gets too hot. When preparing a cheese sauce, stir finely grated cheese into the hot sauce base and leave to stand. The cheese will melt without further cooking. Cheese toppings will not brown except in a combination oven. A medium setting is best for cheese.

Above and left: the number and variety of different baking dishes and the range of equipment for the microwave is vast.

Baking

Baking is one of the most surprising things a microwave oven does. Quick breads, those leavened with baking powder or soda and sour milk, rise higher than they do in a conventional oven and bake faster. If using a square or loaf dish, cover the corners with foil for part of the cooking time to keep that part of the bread or cake from drying out before the middle is cooked. Cakes also rise much higher and a single layer will bake in about 6 minutes on a medium setting.

Microwave ovens can cut the rising time for yeast doughs nearly in half, and a loaf of bread will bake in an astonishing 8-10 minutes.

Biscuits will not usually crisp in a microwave oven except in one with a combination setting. However, they bake to a moist, chewy texture which is just as pleasing. A batch of 3 dozen will cook in about 10 minutes.

Pastry is not as much of a problem as most people believe. Prick the base and sides of the pastry well, after lining a pie or flan dish. It is essential to bake the pastry shell "blind" — without filling — in order to dry the base. Pastry will not bake to an even brown. The exception is, of course, pastry baked in a combination oven. Pastry and filling can be baked at the same time in these ovens.

To let air and heat circulate underneath breads, cakes and pastry shells, place them on a rack or inverted saucer. This allows the base to cook faster and more evenly. Once baked and cool, keep microwave-baked goods well covered. They seem to dry out faster than those conventionally baked.

Defrosting and Reheating

With the defrosting and reheating abilities of a microwave oven menu planning can become crisis-free. Most ovens incorporate an automatic defrosting control into their setting programs. If your oven does not have this facility, use the lowest temperature setting and employ an on/off technique. In other words, turn the oven on at 30 second-1 minute intervals and let the food stand for a minute or two before repeating the process. This

CHART 5 Reheating

	Quantity	Setting	Time from room temp. (minutes)	Special Instructions
Spaghetti Sauce	225g/8oz 450g/1lb	Med.	5-6 7-8	Stir several times. Keep loosely covered.
Pasta	120g/4oz 225g/8oz	Med. or High	2-3 5-6	Stir once or twice. Add 5ml/1 tsp oil. Use shorter time for High setting.
Rice	120g/4oz 225g/8oz	Med. or High	2-3 4-5	Stir once or twice. Add 5ml/1 tsp oil or butter. Use shorter time for High setting.
Potatoes	120g/4oz 225g/8oz 450g/1lb	High	1-2 2-3 3-4	Use the shorter time for mashed potatoes. Do not reheat fried potatoes. Cover loosely.
Corn-on-the-Cob	2 ears 4 ears	High	2-3 4-6	Wrap in plastic wrap/cling film
Carrots	225g/8oz 450g/1lb	High	1-2 2-4	Cover loosely. Stir once.
Turnips	225g/8oz 450g/1lb	High	1-2 2-4	Cover loosely. Stir carefully.
Broccoli Asparagus	120g/4oz 225g/8oz	High	2 2	Cover loosely. Rearrange once.
Peas Beans Courgettes/ Zucchini	120g/4oz 225g/8oz	High	1-1½ 1½-2	Cover loosely. Stir occasionally.

CHART 4 Defrosting

	Mins. on Low/ Defrost Setting per 450g/1lb	Mins. Stdg. Time	Instructions
Vegetables	1-8	3-5	Cover loosely. Break up or stir occasionally.
Bread Loaf	2-4 (per average loaf)	5-10	Cover with paper towels. Turn over once.
1 Slice Bread	20 seconds	1	Cover in paper towels.
Rolls 6 12	1½-3 2-4	3 5	Cover in paper towels. Turn over once.
Cake	1½-2	2	Place on serving plate. Some icings not suitable.
Fruit Pie 23cm/9"	8-10	6	Use a glass dish. Place on inverted saucer or rack.

Always cover the food when defrosting or reheating. Plastic containers, plastic bags and freezer-to-table ware can be used to freeze and defrost food in. Meals can be placed on paper or plastic trays and frozen. Cover with cling film or greaseproof paper. Usually, foods are better defrosted first and cooked or reheated second. There are exceptions to this rule, so be sure to check instructions on pre-packaged foods before proceeding. Food frozen in blocks, such as spinach or casseroles, should be broken up as they defrost.

Breads, rolls and coffee cakes can be placed on paper plates or covered in paper towels to reheat or defrost. These materials will help protect the foods and absorb moisture which will come to the surface and could make these foods soggy. If you want a crisp crust on reheated bread, slip a sheet of foil under the paper towel and don't cover completely.

Foods can be arranged on plates in advance and reheated

procedure allows the food to defrost evenly without starting to cook at the edges. The times given in Charts No. 4 and 5 apply to ovens of 600-700 watts.

CHART 6 Weights and Measures

LIQUID				DRY	
Metric	Imperial	American		Metric	Imperial
30ml	1 fl oz	2 tbsps		30g	1oz
60ml	2 fl oz	4 tbsps/¼ cup		60g	2oz
90ml	3 fl oz	5 tbsps/⅓ cup		90g	3oz
140ml	¼ pint	½ cup		120g	4oz/¼ lb
280ml	½ pint	1 cup		180g	6oz
430ml	¾ pint	1½ cups		225g	8oz/½ lb
570ml	1 pint	2 cups/16 fl oz		250g	9oz
700ml	1¼ pints	2½ cups		340g	12oz/¾ lb
850ml	1½ pints	3 cups		400g	14oz
1 litre	1¾ pints	3½ cups		450g	1lb
1150ml	2 pints	4 cups		560g	1¼ lbs
				675g	1½ lbs
				790g	1¾lbs
				900g	2lbs
				1kg	2¼ lbs

Butter or Margarine	30g/1oz/2 tbsps 120g/4oz/½ cup or 1 stick
Cheese	120g/4oz/1 cup
Dried Beans, etc:	450g/1lb/2¼ cups
Dry Breadcrumbs	120g/4oz/1 cup
Dried Fruit	225g/8oz/1½ cups
Flour	120-150g/4-5oz/1 cup
Nuts	120g/4oz/1 cup
Oatmeal and other Cereals	90g/3oz/1 cup
Pasta Soup Shells	225g/8oz/1½ cups 225g/8oz/3 cups
Powdered/ Icing Sugar	120g/4oz/1 cup
Rice	225g/8oz/2 cups
Sugar	225g/8oz/1 cup

IMPORTANT NOTE: Measurements are NOT exact equivalents

very successfully, an advantage when entertaining. With a microwave oven, you can spend more time with your guests than by yourself in the kitchen!

Recipe Conversion

Experiment with your favourite recipes and you will probably find that many of them can be converted for microwave cooking with only a few changes. Things that don't work are recipes which call for whipped egg whites, such as angel food cake and crisp meringue shells. Soft meringues for pies will work, and one of the most amazing recipe conversions is that for crisp meringues. These meringues triple in size as they cook and are made from a fondant-like mixture.

Batters for pancakes, waffles or Yorkshire pudding are impossible to cook successfully.

To convert your own recipes, the following rules will help:

* Look for similar microwave recipes with the same quantities of solid ingredients, dish size, techniques and times.

* Reduce liquid quantities by one quarter. More can always be added later in cooking.

* Reduce the seasoning in your recipe; microwave cooking intensifies flavours.

* Microwave cooking takes approximately a quarter of the time of conventional cooking. Allow at least 5 minutes standing time before checking to see if the food is cooked. You can always add more time at this point if necessary.

Microwave
THE RECIPES

Microwave
VEGETARIAN
COOKING

The microwave oven has a brilliant way with vegetables. Fast cooking times mean vegetables keep their fresh colour and crisp texture. Low evaporation means vegetables need very little water to cook, so they keep their nutrients. Fresh vegetables cook as quickly as frozen vegetables do by conventional methods, and frozen vegetables are cooked beautifully in almost the blink of an eye.

Vegetarian diets are losing their "cranky" image as more people turn to that way of eating because of weight and nutrition consciousness. The humble dried bean or lentil has an abundant supply of protein to add to our diets, with the added plus of more fibre than many other protein foods.

The microwave method of rehydrating pulses – dried peas, beans and lentils – eliminates overnight soaking. Just cover the dried pulses with water and bring them to the boil, which usually takes about 10 minutes on the highest setting. After that, allow the pulses to boil for 2 minutes. Leave them standing, covered, in the hot water for 1 hour and they will be ready to cook according to your recipe. Dried pulses usually take about an hour to cook. If that doesn't seem like convenience cooking, remember that conventional methods would take twice as long. It is essential, though, that dried peas, beans and lentils are thoroughly cooked. Eating insufficiently cooked pulses can be dangerous.

Vegetarian menus have suffered from the image that they are composed solely of nut cutlets. I have always found that unfair, since well seasoned cutlets are a delicious alternative to meat and a good addition to a healthy diet. Nut cutlets, escalopes and croquettes are very easy to cook in a microwave oven with the use of a browning dish. Be creative with shapes, too, because nut mixtures hold up better in a microwave oven than they do when fried or baked conventionally.

When organising the recipes into chapters, I was amazed to find just how many recipes could fit easily in several different categories. Pulses can be used in salads, appetizers or entrées. Main courses can be cut down and used as appetizers and appetizers can be expanded to main-meal-sized portions. Even desserts and puddings can be based on vegetables. Which all goes to prove that, vegetarian or not, we can all enjoy more creative meals thanks to the versatility of vegetables.

APPETIZERS

Tomato and Tarragon Creams with Sweetcorn Salad

PREPARATION TIME: 25 minutes

MICROWAVE COOKING TIME: 9-10 minutes

SERVES: 4 people

400g/14oz plum tomatoes, canned
30ml/2 tbsps tomato purée/paste
1 onion, finely chopped
5ml/1 tsp chopped tarragon
1 bay leaf
Salt and pepper
225g/8oz low fat or cream cheese
2 eggs
280ml/½ pint/1 cup whipped cream
15g/½ oz/1 tbsp gelatine or agar-agar
45ml/3 tbsps water and lemon juice mixed
Salt and pepper

SALAD
225g/8oz/baby corn-on-the-cob
1 green pepper, cut in thin strips
4-6 tomatoes, peeled, seeded and cut in strips
4-6 spring/green onions, shredded
45ml/3 tbsps salad oil
15ml/1 tbsp white wine vinegar
5ml/1 tsp white wine vinegar
5ml/1 tsp Dijon mustard
5ml/1 tsp chopped fresh tarragon
Lettuce leaves

GARNISH
Whole tarragon leaves

Sprinkle the gelatine on top of the water and lemon juice in a small ramekin/custard cup. If using agar-agar in leaf form, dissolve with the water or lemon juice in a small cup. Combine the tomatoes, onion, tarragon, bay leaf, tomato purée/ paste, salt and pepper in a deep bowl. Cook, uncovered, 5 minutes on HIGH. Sieve the pulp and set it aside to cool. Beat the eggs and cheese together until smooth. Add the

This page: Tomato and Tarragon Creams with Sweetcorn Salad. Facing Page: Danish Egg Salad (top) and Pasta and Asparagus Salad (bottom).

cooled tomato pulp. Melt the gelatine or agar-agar for 30 seconds on HIGH. Pour into the tomato mixture and stir well. Set briefly over ice and stir constantly until beginning to thicken. Fold in the cream and adjust the seasoning. Brush 4 ramekin dishes/custard cups lightly with oil and spoon in the tomato mixture. Chill until firm. Put the corn into a large bowl with enough hot water to cover. Cover loosely and cook for 3-4 minutes on HIGH until tender. After 2-3 minutes add the pepper strips. Remove the vegetables with a slotted spoon and rinse under cold water. Set aside to drain. Put the tomatoes into the same water and cook 30 seconds on HIGH. Put into cold water immediately. Remove the skins, cut in half and scoop out the seeds. Slice the flesh into thin strips. Mix the oil, vinegar, tarragon, salt and pepper and combine with the vegetables. Add the spring/green onions just before serving. Arrange lettuce leaves on serving plates and carefully turn out the tomato creams. It may be necessary to dip the moulds briefly into hot water to loosen. Decorate the creams with whole tarragon leaves and serve surrounded with the corn salad.

Danish Egg Salad

PREPARATION TIME: 20 minutes
MICROWAVE COOKING TIME: 7 minutes
SERVES: 4 people

4 eggs
30ml/2 tbsps cream
30g/1oz/2 tbsps butter or margarine
225g/8oz/1 cup frozen peas, thawed
1 cucumber, cut into 1.25cm/½ inch dice
6 sticks of celery, diced
3 spring onions, chopped
30ml/2 tbsps chopped dill
120g/4oz/1 cup diced cheese
280ml/½ pint/1 cup sour cream
60ml/2 fl oz/¼ cup mayonnaise
Paprika
Salt and pepper
1 head Chinese cabbage/leaves, shredded

Beat the eggs and cream together with salt and pepper. Heat a browning dish 5 minutes on HIGH, melt the butter or margarine for 1 minute on HIGH. Pour in half the egg mixture and cook the omelette on one side for 1 minute on HIGH. Turn over and cook a further 1 minute. Cook the egg in two batches. Cook the peas for 1 minute on HIGH with 2 tbsps water. Rinse under cold water and drain to dry. Mix the sour cream, mayonnaise, dill, salt and pepper together. Reserve 30ml/ 2 tbsps dressing and mix the remaining dressing with the peas, celery, cheese and cucumber. Arrange the Chinese cabbage/leaves on serving plates. Pile on the salad. Cut the omelettes into strips and arrange on top. Drizzle the remaining dressing over the omelette strips and sprinkle with paprika.

Warm Salad with Avocado, Grapes, Blue Cheese and Walnuts

PREPARATION TIME: 20 minutes
MICROWAVE COOKING TIME: 1-2 minutes
SERVES: 4 people

1 head curly endive
1 head Belgian endive (chicory)
1 head radicchio
1 small bunch lambs lettuce or watercress
1 head Chinese leaves/cabbage
1 head leaf or iceberg lettuce
4 tbsps chopped fresh herbs
120g/4oz/1 cup walnuts
120g/4oz/1 cup blue cheese crumbled
1 large or 2 small avocados
1 small bunch purple/black grapes

DRESSING
90ml/6 tbsps walnut oil and grapeseed oil mixed
30ml/2 tbsps lemon vinegar or white wine vinegar and lemon juice mixed
Pinch sugar

Tear the curly endive, Belgian endive, radicchio and lettuce into small pieces. If using lambs lettuce separate the leaves. If using watercress remove any thick stalks. Shred the Chinese leaves/cabbage and peel and slice the avocado. Cut the grapes in half and remove any seeds/pips. Combine all the salad ingredients in a large bowl. Mix the salad dressing ingredients and toss with the salad. Arrange on individual salad plates and heat each plate for 1-2 minutes on HIGH before serving.

Pasta and Asparagus Salad

PREPARATION TIME: 15 minutes
MICROWAVE COOKING TIME: 11 minutes plus 8 minutes standing time
SERVES: 4 people

120g/4oz tagliatelle/fettuccine
450g/1lb asparagus, trimmed and cut into 5cm/2 inch pieces
2 courgettes/zucchini, cut into 5cm/ 2 inch sticks
1 lemon, peeled and segmented
30g/2 tbsps chopped parsley
30g/2 tbsps chopped marjoram
Grated rind and juice of 1 lemon
90ml/3 fl oz/⅓ cup salad oil
Pinch sugar (optional)
Salt and pepper
1 head lettuce
1 head Belgian endive (chicory)

Put the pasta into a large bowl with 570ml/1 pint/2 cups hot water, a pinch of salt and 5ml/1 tsp oil. Cook 6 minutes on HIGH and leave to stand in the water for 8 minutes. Drain and leave to cool completely. Cook the asparagus in 140ml/ ¼ pint/½ cup water for 5 minutes on HIGH or until tender. Add the courgettes/zucchini after 3 minutes cooking time. Rinse under cold water and drain. Combine the pasta, asparagus, courgettes/zucchini, parsley, marjoram and lemon segments in a large bowl. Mix the lemon rind, juice, oil, salt and pepper together to blend well. Pour over the

Facing page: Warm Salad with Avocado, Grapes, Blue Cheese and Walnuts.

combined ingredients and toss to coat. Arrange lettuce and endive on serving plates and pile on the salad to serve.

Eggs Primavera

PREPARATION TIME: 20 minutes

MICROWAVE COOKING TIME: 12-14 minutes

SERVES: 4 people

4 eggs
120g/4oz peapods/mangetout
2 large carrots
225g/8oz asparagus
1 small cauliflower
4 spring onions/green onions
1 small head Chinese leaves/cabbage, shredded

DRESSING
280ml/½ pint/1 cup yogurt
1 ripe avocado
140ml/¼ pint/½ cup cream

Put 570ml/1 pint/2½ cups water in a shallow dish with 15ml/1tbsp vinegar and 5ml/1 tsp salt. Heat the water on HIGH for 3-4 minutes or until boiling. Break the eggs one at a time into a cup and slide them into the water. Pierce the yolks once with a small knife or skewer. Cover the dish loosely and cook for 2-3 minutes on MEDIUM. When the whites are set lift the eggs out of the dish and put them immediately into a bowl of cold water. Trim the asparagus spears and cut them into 5cm/2 inch pieces. Separate the head of cauliflower into individual flowerets. Put the asparagus into a casserole with 30ml/2 tbsps water. Cook for 5 minutes on HIGH. After 1 minute add flowerets of cauliflower. Three minutes before the end of cooking time add the mangetout/peapods and the carrots, cut into ribbons with a vegetable peeler. Leave the vegetables to stand, covered, for 1 minute and then rinse under cold water and dry well. Slice the spring/green onions and add to the rest of the vegetables. Pile the Chinese leaves/cabbage onto 4 individual plates. Put the mixed vegetables on top. Drain the poached eggs well and put 1 egg on top of each

salad. Peel the avocado and combine with the yogurt in a food processor and purée until smooth. Stir in the cream and season with salt and pepper. Coat some of the dressing over each egg and serve the rest separately.

Red Pepper Pâté in Lemon Shells

PREPARATION TIME: 20 minutes

MICROWAVE COOKING TIME: 8-9 minutes

SERVES: 4 people

4 lemons, cut in half
6 red peppers, cored, seeded and cut in pieces
60ml/2 fl oz/4 tbsps white wine
1 bay leaf
450g/1lb cream cheese
½ chili pepper, finely chopped
Pinch ground oregano
Salt
Pinch sugar (optional)

This page: Red Pepper Pâté in Lemon Shells. Facing page: Oeufs à la Russe (top) and Eggs Primavera (bottom).

GARNISH
8 thin slices of red pepper
8 small fresh bay leaves
Chinese cabbage/leaves, shredded

ACCOMPANIMENT
Melba or hot buttered toast

Scoop out the pulp from the lemon. Squeeze the juice and set it aside. Trim a slice from the bottom of each lemon half so that they stand upright. Combine peppers, wine and bay leaf in a medium size casserole. Cover and cook 8-10 minutes on HIGH until very soft. Remove the bay leaf and purée the peppers and wine in a food processor. Add the cream cheese, chili pepper, oregano, salt, lemon juice and sugar (if using). Process until smooth. Adjust the seasoning and pipe or spoon the pâté into the lemon shells. Chill briefly

aside. Chop the mushroom stalks and combine with the walnuts, pimento, chives, mustard, salt, pepper and breadcrumbs. Add any cooking liquid from the mushrooms and the beaten egg. Mound the filling onto the mushroom caps. Cook on MEDIUM for 6-8 minutes until the filling is set. Mix the topping ingredients and spoon onto the mushroom filling. Cook a further 2 minutes on MEDIUM or 3 minutes on a combination setting of a microwave convection oven. Serve immediately. The cheese topping may be sprinkled lightly with paprika before the final cooking if desired.

Spinach-Stuffed Artichoke Hearts

PREPARATION TIME: 25 minutes

MICROWAVE COOKING TIME: 19-20 minutes

SERVES: 4 people

4 globe artichokes
450g/1lb fresh spinach, stalks removed and well washed
1 shallot finely chopped
1 egg, beaten
140ml/¼ pint/½ cup heavy/double cream
2 slices bread, made into crumbs
15g/½ oz/1 tbsp butter or margarine
Nutmeg
Cayenne pepper
Salt

TOPPING
60g/2oz/½ cup grated Cheddar cheese
60ml/4 tbsps heavy/double cream

Cut all of the top leaves off the artichokes. Trim the remaining leaves down to the thickest part. Cut out as much of the choke as possible. Cover the artichokes with water and cook in a covered casserole for 7-8 minutes on HIGH. Drain well and remove any remaining choke. Trim the remaining leaves down further until

This page: Spinach-Stuffed Artichoke Hearts (top) and Stuffed Mushrooms (bottom). Facing page: Aubergine/Eggplant Caviar (top) and Avocado, Tomato and Mozzarella on Garlic Toast (bottom).

before serving. Garnish each with a slice of red pepper and one bay leaf. Arrange on a bed of Chinese cabbage/leaves. Serve with hot buttered toast or melba toast.

Stuffed Mushrooms

PREPARATION TIME: 15 minutes

MICROWAVE COOKING TIME: 8-11 minutes

SERVES: 4 people

4 very large or 8 medium-size mushrooms
30g/2 tbsps butter
3 slices white bread, made into crumbs
120g/4oz/1 cup chopped walnuts
3 pimento caps, chopped
1 egg, beaten
1 small bunch chives, snipped
15ml/1 tbsp Dijon mustard
Salt and pepper

TOPPING
30g/1oz/2 tbsps cream cheese
15g/½ oz/1 tbsp grated Gruyère or Cheddar cheese
90ml/3 fl oz/⅓ cup heavy/double cream
Pinch cayenne pepper

Melt the butter in a large, shallow dish. Remove the stalks from the mushrooms and set them aside. Cook the whole mushroom caps for 2 minutes on HIGH, remove and set

only the thick, edible part remains. Cook the spinach in the water that clings to the leaves on HIGH for 5 minutes. Melt the butter 30 seconds on HIGH in a small bowl. Cook the shallot for 1 minute until softenend. Combine with the spinach, breadcrumbs, egg, cream, nutmeg, cayenne pepper and salt. Mound the filling onto the artichoke bottoms. Arrange in a circle and cook 5 minutes on MEDIUM or until set. Mix the topping ingredients together and spoon onto the spinach filling. Cook a further 2 minutes on MEDIUM to melt the cheese, or for 3 minutes on a combination setting in a microwave convection oven. Sprinkle lightly with more grated nutmeg before serving.

Courgette/Zucchini and Carrot Terrine

PREPARATION TIME: 20 minutes

MICROWAVE COOKING TIME: 17 minutes plus 10 minutes standing time

SERVES: 4-6 people

6-8 large, green cabbage leaves
340g/12oz low fat cheese
4 slices bread, made into crumbs
2 eggs
140ml/¼ pint/½ cup cream, lightly whipped
1 bunch chives, snipped
Salt and pepper
1-2 carrots, cut in strips
1-2 courgettes/zucchini, cut in strips

SAUCE
280ml/½ pint/1 cup sour cream or plain yogurt
140ml/¼ pint/½ cup mayonnaise
2 tomatoes, peeled, seeded and cut in small dice
30ml/2 tbsps chopped parsley
15ml/1 tbsp lemon juice or white wine
Pinch sugar (optional)
Salt and pepper

Trim the spines of the cabbage leaves to make them thinner. Place the leaves in a shallow dish with 30ml/ 2 tbsps water and a pinch of salt. Cover the dish loosely and cook for

1 minute on HIGH. Line a 450g/1lb loaf dish with the cabbage leaves. Mix together the cheese, breadcrumbs, eggs, cream, chives and salt and pepper. Cook the carrots in 30ml/2 tbsps water for 5 minutes on HIGH. Add the courgettes after 3 minutes cooking time. Drain and dry both vegetables very well. Put a quarter of the mixture into the bottom of the loaf dish on top of the cabbage leaves. Place on 1 layer of carrots and cover with another quarter of the cheese mixture. Place on a layer of courgettes and repeat the process until all the mixture and the vegetables are used. Wrap over the overlapping cabbage leaves. Cover the dish with the cling film/ plastic wrap, pierce several times to release the steam. Put into the microwave oven with a small dish of hot water and cook for 10 minutes on MEDIUM. Allow to cool in the dish. Combine the sauce ingredients. Slice the terrine and arrange on lettuce leaves or watercress. Spoon over some of the sauce and serve the rest separately.

Aubergine/Eggplant Caviar

PREPARATION TIME: 20 minutes

MICROWAVE COOKING TIME: 7-9 minutes

SERVES: 4 people

1 large or 2 small aubergines/eggplants
60ml/4 tbsps oil
Juice of ½ lemon
1 clove garlic, minced
Pinch cayenne pepper
Salt

GARNISH
2 hard boiled eggs
1 small onion, finely chopped
30g/2 tbsps chopped parsley
4-8 slices French bread, toasted

Remove the stem from the eggplant/ aubergine, cut it in half and lightly score the flesh. Sprinkle with salt and leave to stand for 30 minutes to draw out any bitterness. Rinse and pat dry. Put into a covered casserole and

cook on HIGH for 7-9 minutes. Allow to cool and cut into small pieces. Combine in a food processor with the garlic, lemon juice, salt and pepper. Blend until smooth. Pour the oil gradually through the feedtube with the machine running. Adjust the seasoning and chill. Sieve the egg yolk and finely chop the white. To serve, pile the aubergine/eggplant caviar on top of the French bread toast and sprinkle on the onion, egg and parsley.

Oeufs à la Russe

PREPARATION TIME: 20 minutes

MICROWAVE COOKING TIME: 35-40 minutes plus 10 minutes standing time

SERVES: 4 people

4 eggs
3 beetroot/beets
120g/4oz mushrooms
4 sticks celery
2-3 potatoes, depending on size
15ml/1 tbsp butter or margarine
180g/6oz fresh spinach

DRESSING
430ml/¾ pint/1½ cups sour cream
5ml/1 tsp white wine vinegar
2.5ml/½ tsp sugar
1 bunch chives, chopped
Salt and pepper

Poach the eggs as for Eggs Primavera. Leave in cold water until ready to use. Put the beetroot/beets into a deep bowl with 140ml/¼ pint/½ cup water and a pinch of salt. Cover the bowl loosely with cling film/plastic wrap and cook on HIGH for 12-16 minutes, stirring once or twice. Remove the beetroot/beets from the bowl and set aside to stand 10 minutes before peeling. Rinse out the bowl and add the potatoes cut in 1.25cm/½ inch dice. Add 140ml/ ¼ pint/½ cup water and a pinch of

Facing page: Broccoli and Hazelnut Terrine (top) and Courgette/ Zucchini and Carrot Terrine (bottom).

salt and cover the bowl loosely with cling film/plastic wrap. Cook the potatoes on HIGH for 8-10 minutes, stirring once. Leave to stand while preparing the rest of the salad. Heat the butter in a small bowl for 30 seconds on HIGH and add the mushrooms, quartered, and the celery, cut in small dice. Cook for 1 minute on HIGH, stirring occasionally. Drain the potatoes and add them to the celery and mushrooms. Leave to cool. Combine the dressing ingredients and set them aside. Wash the spinach leaves well and dry and shred them finely. Add 60ml/2 fl oz/¼ cup of the dressing to the potatoes, celery and mushrooms and stir to coat. Add the beetroot/beets and stir very carefully. Pile the salad onto the spinach and top each salad with 1 drained poached egg. Coat the remaining dressing over each egg before serving.

Avocado, Tomato and Mozzarella on Garlic Toast

PREPARATION TIME: 15 minutes

MICROWAVE COOKING TIME: 9 minutes

SERVES: 4 people

4 slices French or Vienna bread, sliced
* 1.25cm/½ inch thick, on the diagonal*
60g/2oz/4 tbsps butter or margarine
15ml/1 tbsp oil
1 clove garlic, crushed
2-4 beefsteak tomatoes
1-2 ripe avocados
120g/4oz mozzarella cheese, sliced
30ml/2 tbsps capers
30ml/2 tbsps salad oil
10ml/2 tsps lemon juice
2.5ml/½ tsp oregano
Salt and pepper

Heat a browning dish for 5 minutes on HIGH. Add the oil, butter and garlic. Put in the bread slices, two at a time if necessary. Brown for 1 minute on HIGH and turn over. Cook another 1 minute on HIGH and set on paper towels to drain. Peel the avocados, remove the stones and slice. Slice the tomatoes and the

cheese and arrange on top of the bread slices, alternating with the avocado slices. Scatter over the capers. Mix the oil, lemon juice, oregano, salt and pepper and spoon on top. Heat 2 minutes on MEDIUM to melt the cheese. Serve immediately.

Salad of Wild Mushrooms and Artichokes

PREPARATION TIME: 20 minutes

MICROWAVE COOKING TIME: 9-11 minutes

SERVES: 4 people

2-3 globe artichokes, depending on size
1 slice lemon
1 bay leaf
6 black peppercorns
225g/8oz oyster mushrooms (other
* varieties of wild mushrooms may be*
* substituted)*
30ml/2 tbsps oil
1 head radicchio (red or Italian lettuce)
1 head iceberg or leaf lettuce
1 bunch watercress
1 small bunch fresh chives, snipped

DRESSING
90ml/6 tbsps oil
30ml/2 tbsps white wine vinegar
15ml/1 tbsp Dijon mustard
Salt and pepper

GARNISH
Fresh chervil or dill

Trim the tips of the artichoke leaves. Put the artichokes into a large bowl with the lemon, bay leaf, peppercorns and enough water to cover. Cook 7-8 minutes or until the bottom leaf pulls away easily. Drain upside-down. Remove the stalks and slice the mushrooms thickly. Cook for 1-2 minutes in 30ml/2 tbsps oil and set aside. Tear the radicchio and lettuce into small pieces. Add the watercress leaves and toss together with the chives. Mix the salad dressing ingredients together until very well blended. Remove the leaves of the artichokes and arrange them on 4 plates. Top with the radicchio and watercress. Remove the chokes from

the artichoke hearts and discard. Cut the artichoke hearts into thin slices and combine with the mushrooms. Toss with half of the dressing, spoon equal amounts over the salads. Reheat each for 1 minute on HIGH. Garnish with the chervil and serve the remaining dressing separately.

Broccoli and Hazelnut Terrine

PREPARATION TIME: 20 minutes

MICROWAVE COOKING TIME: 10 minutes plus 10 minutes standing time

SERVES: 4-6 people

6-8 large or 12-14 small whole spinach
* leaves*
450g/1lb broccoli
1 shallot, finely chopped
180g/6oz/¾ cup low fat cheese
4 slices bread, made into fine crumbs
2 eggs
280ml/½ pint/1 cup cream, lightly
* whipped*
120g/4oz/1 cup coarsely chopped,
* roasted hazelnuts*
Pinch nutmeg
Pinch thyme
Salt and pepper

SAUCE
280ml/½ pint/1 cup mayonnaise
140ml/¼ pint/½ cup plain yogurt
Grated rind and juice of 1 lemon
Pinch cayenne pepper
Salt

Trim away any coarse stalks from the spinach but leave the leaves whole. Wash them well and put them into a shallow dish with a pinch of salt. Loosely cover the dish and cook for 1 minute on HIGH with only the water that clings to the leaves. Remove from the dish and press on paper towels to drain. Line a 450g/1lb loaf dish with the spinach leaves and set aside. Chop the broccoli finely. Mix the eggs, cheese, cream, breadcrumbs, shallot, thyme, nutmeg and salt and pepper together. Stir in the broccoli and the hazelnuts. Spoon the mixture into the loaf dish on top of the spinach leaves and pack down well.

Fold the spinach leaves over on top of the mixture. Cover the dish with 2 layers of cling film/plastic wrap, pierced several times to let out steam. Put a ramekin/custard cup of water into the microwave oven with the terrine and cook on MEDIUM for 10 minutes or until just barely set. Allow to cool in the dish. Mix the sauce ingredients together. Turn the terrine out of the dish and slice. Arrange on lettuce leaves or

This page: Salad of Wild Mushrooms and Artichokes.

radicchio (red or Italian lettuce) and spoon over some of the sauce. Serve the remaining sauce separately.

VEGETABLE SOUPS

Cream of Watercress Soup

PREPARATION TIME: 20 minutes

MICROWAVE COOKING TIME:
12-13 minutes plus 5 minutes
standing time

SERVES: 4 people

2 medium potatoes, cut in even-size
    pieces
3 bunches watercress, well washed and
    root ends removed
1 litre/1¾ pints/3½ cups vegetable stock
Juice of ½ lemon
1.25ml/¼ tsp ground nutmeg
280ml-430ml/½-¾ pint/1-1½ cups
    single/light cream
Salt and pepper

GARNISH
120ml/4 tbsps heavy/double cream
Reserved watercress leaves

Put the stock and the potatoes into a
large bowl with a pinch of salt.
Partially cover and cook for 10
minutes on HIGH or until the
potatoes are tender. Allow to stand
for 5 minutes. Add the lemon juice,
salt, pepper, watercress and nutmeg
and purée in a food processor until
smooth. Stir in the cream and
process once more. Heat 2-3 minutes
on HIGH before serving. Garnish
with a swirl of cream and the
reserved watercress leaves.

Tomato and Dill Bisque

PREPARATION TIME: 20 minutes

MICROWAVE COOKING TIME:
7½ minutes

SERVES: 4 people

900g/2lbs tomatoes
850ml/1½ pints/3 cups vegetable stock
30ml/2 tbsps tomato purée/paste
1 onion, peeled and chopped
2 sprigs fresh dill
Salt and pepper
10ml/2 tsps chopped fresh dill
140ml/¼ pint/½ cup double/heavy
    cream

This page: Beetroot and Sour
Cream Soup with Horseradish.
Facing page: Tomato and Dill
Bisque (top) and Cream of
Watercress Soup (bottom).

GARNISH
1 slice tomato
4 small sprigs fresh dill
60ml/2 fl oz/¼ cup plain yogurt

Cut half of 1 cucumber into small dice and set aside. Peel the other half and the remaining 2 cucumbers and chop them roughly. Place the cucumbers in a large bowl with the stock and salt and pepper. Remove the mint leaves from the stalks and add the stalks to the cucumbers. Cover the bowl loosely and cook 6 minutes on HIGH or until the cucumbers are tender. Remove the mint stalks and purée the soup in a food processor. Strain if desired and add the cream and cucumber dice. Re-heat for 2 minutes on HIGH. Chop the mint leaves just before serving and add to the soup. Garnish with yogurt.

Sweetcorn and Red Pepper Soup

PREPARATION TIME: 20 minutes

MICROWAVE COOKING TIME: 14 minutes plus 5 minutes standing time

SERVES: 4 people

4 medium potatoes, cut in even-size
    pieces
570ml/1 pint/2 cups vegetable stock
225g/8oz/1½ cups corn/sweetcorn
1 bay leaf
15ml/1 tbsp butter or margarine
1 red chili pepper
1 large, sweet red pepper
1 onion, chopped
Salt and pepper
570ml/1 pint/2 cups milk

GARNISH
Chopped parsley

Pour the stock into a large bowl and add the potatoes, bay leaf and a pinch of salt. Partially cover and cook 10 minutes on HIGH or until the potatoes are tender. Leave to stand for 5 minutes and remove the bay leaf. Purée until smooth. Melt the butter 30 seconds on HIGH and

Cut the tomatoes in half, remove the seeds and strain the juice into a large bowl. Add the onion, sprigs of dill, tomato purée/paste, halved tomatoes, salt, pepper and stock. Partially cover and cook on HIGH for 7 minutes or until the tomatoes have broken down and the onions are soft. Remove the sprigs of dill and pour the soup into a food processor. Purée the soup until smooth, and strain to remove any tomato skins. Adjust the seasoning and add a pinch of sugar if necessary to bring out the tomato flavour. Stir in the cream and chopped dill and re-heat for 30 seconds on HIGH. Garnish each serving with a spoonful of yogurt, a tomato strip and a sprig of fresh dill.

Cream of Cucumber Soup with Mint

PREPARATION TIME: 20 minutes

MICROWAVE COOKING TIME: 7-8 minutes plus 5 minutes standing time

SERVES: 4 people

3 large cucumbers (seedless variety)
1 litre/1¾ pints/3½ cups vegetable stock
2-3 sprigs mint
280ml/½ pint/1 cup single/light cream
Salt and pepper

GARNISH
Cucumber dice
60ml/2 fl oz/¼ cup plain yogurt

This page: Sweetcorn and Red Pepper Soup. Facing page: Cream of Cucumber Soup with Mint (top) and Fresh Pea Soup with Thyme (bottom).

cook the onion, pepper, and chili pepper for 2 minutes on HIGH. Add to the puréed potato along with the corn/sweetcorn and milk. Cook 2 minutes on HIGH and adjust the seasoning. Garnish with chopped parsley.

Purée of Asparagus Soup

PREPARATION TIME: 15 minutes

MICROWAVE COOKING TIME: 11 minutes plus 5 minutes standing time

SERVES: 4 people

1340g/3lbs asparagus
1 litre/1¾ pints/3½ cups vegetable stock
1.25ml/¼ tsp ground mace
280ml/½ pint/1 cup single/light cream
Salt and pepper

GARNISH
140ml/¼ pint/½ cup whipped cream, unsweetened
Ground mace

Trim the thick ends of the asparagus and chop the spears to even-sized pieces. Place in a large bowl with the stock, mace, salt and pepper. Partially cover and cook 10 minutes on HIGH or until the asparagus is soft. Leave to stand for 5 minutes. Purée in a food processor and strain if desired. Add the cream and heat 1 minute on HIGH. Garnish each serving with a spoonful of whipped cream and sprinkle with mace.

Fresh Pea Soup with Thyme

PREPARATION TIME: 20 minutes

MICROWAVE COOKING TIME: 7-13 minutes

SERVES: 4 people

1.8kg/4lbs fresh peas, shelled (1.3kg/3lbs frozen peas may be substituted)
1 litre/1¾ pints/3½ cups vegetable stock
2 sprigs fresh thyme
280ml/½ pint/1 cup single/light cream
Salt and pepper

GARNISH
140ml/¼ pint/½ cup heavy/double cream
Reserved peas

Place the peas in a large bowl with the stock, thyme, salt and pepper. Partially cover and cook for 10 minutes on HIGH or until the peas are soft. If using frozen peas, cook for 5 minutes on HIGH. Leave to stand for 5 minutes. Remove the thyme and discard. Remove about 60g/ 4 tbsps peas to reserve for garnish. Purée the remaining peas and stock in a food processor until smooth. Strain the soup if desired. Stir in the cream and adjust the seasoning. Add the reserved peas and re-heat 2-3 minutes on HIGH. Before serving, swirl a spoonful of cream through each bowl.

Beetroot and Sour Cream Soup with Horseradish

PREPARATION TIME: 20 minutes

MICROWAVE COOKING TIME: 22-23 minutes plus 10 minutes standing time

SERVES: 4 people

225g/8oz turnips, peeled and cut in even-size pieces
450g/1lb beetroot/beets
1 litre/1¾ pints/3½ cups vegetable stock
1 bay leaf
Salt and pepper
280ml/½ pint/1 cup sour cream
15ml/1 tbsp grated fresh or bottled horseradish

GARNISH
Chopped chives
Reserved sour cream

Cook unpeeled beetroot/beets in a large bowl, covered, with 60ml/ 2 fl oz/¼ cup stock for 10 minutes on HIGH. Leave to stand for 10 minutes before peeling. Pre-cooked or canned beetroot may be substituted. Cut into small pieces and return to the bowl with the turnips, remaining stock, bay leaf, salt and pepper. Partially cover the bowl and cook for

a further 10 minutes on HIGH. Remove the bay leaf and purée the soup in a food processor until smooth. Reserve 60ml/4 tbsps sour cream and add the rest to the soup along with the horseradish. Heat 2-3 minutes on MEDIUM. Do not allow the soup to boil. Serve topped with sour cream and chopped chives.

Lettuce Cream Soup with Coriander

PREPARATION TIME: 20 minutes

MICROWAVE COOKING TIME: 15-16 minutes plus 5 minutes standing time

SERVES: 4 people

2 medium-sized potatoes, cut into even-size pieces
1 litre/1¾ pints/3½ cups vegetable stock
2 small heads lettuce, washed and shredded
2.5ml/½ tsp ground coriander
280ml-430ml/½-¾ pint/1-1½ cups single/light cream
Salt and pepper

GARNISH
Reserved shredded lettuce
Chopped parsley

Place the potatoes, stock and a pinch of salt in a large bowl. Partially cover the bowl and cook 10 minutes on HIGH or until the potatoes are tender. Add the lettuce, reserving about a quarter for garnish. Add the coriander and pepper and cook a further 3 minutes on HIGH. Leave to stand 5 minutes before blending in a food processor until smooth. Add 280ml/½ pint/1 cup cream (add more cream if the soup is too thick). The soup should be the consistency of lightly-whipped cream. Add the reserved shredded lettuce and parsley and re-heat for 2-3 minutes on HIGH.

Facing page: Lettuce Cream Soup with Coriander (top) and Purée of Asparagus Soup (bottom).

Mushroom and Sherry Cream Soup

PREPARATION TIME: 20 minutes

MICROWAVE COOKING TIME:
9-11 minutes plus 5 minutes standing time

SERVES: 4 people

900g/2lbs mushrooms, chopped
5-6 slices bread, crust removed
700ml/1¼ pints/2½ cups vegetable stock
1 sprig fresh thyme
1 bay leaf
½ clove garlic, crushed (optional)
430ml/¾ pint/1½ cups light/single
  cream
60ml/2 fl oz/¼ cup sherry
Salt and pepper

GARNISH
140ml/¼ pint/½ cup whipped cream
Grated nutmeg

Combine the mushrooms, bread, stock, thyme, bay leaf, salt, pepper and garlic (if using) in a large bowl. Partially cover and cook on HIGH for 7-8 minutes. Leave to stand for 5 minutes. Remove the thyme and the bay leaf and purée in a food processor until smooth. If the soup is not thick enough, add 1-2 slices more bread with the crusts removed. Add the sherry and process once more. Re-heat 2-3 minutes on HIGH. Garnish each bowl with a spoonful of whipped cream and a sprinkling of nutmeg.

Purée of Leek and Potato Soup

PREPARATION TIME: 20 minutes

MICROWAVE COOKING TIME:
12 minutes plus 5 minutes standing time

SERVES: 4 people

3 medium-size potatoes, cut in even-size
  pieces
4 leeks, depending on size
1 litre/1¾ pints/3½ cups vegetable stock
1 bay leaf
2 sprigs thyme
1.25ml/¼ tsp ground nutmeg

Salt and pepper
280-430ml/½-¾ pint/1-1½ cups single/
  light cream

Wash leeks well and shred the light green portion of 1 of the leeks and reserve. Slice the remaining leeks and combine with the potatoes in a large bowl. Pour on the stock and add the bay leaf, thyme and a pinch of salt. Partially cover the bowl and cook on HIGH for 10 minutes or until the potatoes and leeks are tender. Leave to stand for 5 minutes. Remove the bay leaf and thyme and purée the soup in a food processor until smooth. Add the nutmeg, pepper

This page: Purée of Leek and Potato Soup (top) and Mushroom and Sherry Cream Soup (bottom). Facing page: Spring Vegetable Soup.

and 280ml/½ pint/1 cup cream. Process again and add more cream if the soup is too thick. It should be the consistency of lightly whipped cream. Put the reserved leek into a small dish with 30ml/2 tbsps water and cook for 2 minutes on HIGH. Drain and garnish the soup with a spoonful of sour cream and the reserved leek strips.

Purée of Carrot Soup

PREPARATION TIME: 20 minutes

MICROWAVE COOKING TIME:
16-17 minutes

SERVES: 4 people

1340g/3lbs carrots, scraped and grated
1 litre/1¾ pints/3½ cups vegetable stock
2-3 sprigs rosemary
280ml/½ pint/1 cup milk or light/single
*   cream*
Salt and pepper

GARNISH
140ml/¼ pint/½ cup unsweetened
*   whipped cream*
Chopped parsley

Combine the carrots, rosemary, salt, pepper and stock in a large bowl. Partially cover and cook 15 minutes on HIGH or until the carrots are very tender. Remove the rosemary and purée the soup in a food processor. Add the milk or cream and process until smooth. Adjust the seasoning and re-heat 1-2 minutes on HIGH before serving. Top with spoonfuls of whipped cream and chopped parsley.

Spring Vegetable Soup

PREPARATION TIME: 25 minutes

MICROWAVE COOKING TIME:
30 minutes plus 15-20 minutes standing time

SERVES: 4-6 people

VEGETABLE STOCK
225g/8oz carrots, roughly chopped
6 sticks celery, roughly chopped
1 turnip, roughly chopped (optional)
3 onions, chopped and the peel of 1
*   reserved for colour*
1 tomato, quartered and seeded
3 parsley stalks
1 whole clove
1 bay leaf
1 blade mace
2 sprigs thyme or other fresh herbs
6 black peppercorns
Pinch salt
1150ml/2 pints/4 cups water

SOUP
1 litre/1¾ pint/3½ cups vegetable stock
1 head green cabbage, shredded
120g/4oz asparagus cut in 2.5cm/1 inch
*   pieces*
120g/4oz French/green beans cut in
*   2.5cm/1 inch pieces*
3 carrots, cut in 5cm/2 inch strips
120g/4oz fresh or frozen peas
1 large red pepper, thinly sliced
3 spring/green onions, sliced
60ml/2 fl oz/¼ cup white wine, optional
Salt and pepper

Combine all the ingredients for the stock in a large bowl. Half cover the bowl with cling film/plastic wrap and cook 15 minutes on HIGH. The stock will boil, so the bowl must be deep enough to contain it. Allow to stand for 15-20 minutes before straining. The stock will keep up to 3 days in the refrigerator or frozen in

This page: Purée of Carrot Soup. Facing page: French/Green Beans with Lemon Herb Sauce (top) and Asparagus Tied with Fresh Herbs (bottom).

ice cube trays for convenience. To prepare the soup, pour the measured stock into a large bowl. If using fresh peas add them to the stock and partially cover the bowl. Cook the peas for 5 minutes on HIGH. Add the carrots and cook a further 5 minutes on HIGH. Add the beans, asparagus and cabbage and cook for 5 minutes further on HIGH. Add the onions, peppers and wine after 2 minutes cooking time. If using frozen peas, add them with the onions and peppers. Season with salt and pepper to taste before serving. If preparing the soup in advance, re-heat it for 5-6 minutes on HIGH before serving.

SIDE DISHES

French/Green Beans with Lemon Herb Sauce

PREPARATION TIME: 10 minutes

MICROWAVE COOKING TIME: 7 minutes

SERVES: 4 people

450g/1lb French /green beans
60ml/4 fl oz/¼ cup water
Salt

SAUCE
280ml/½ pint/1 cup low fat soft cheese
 or fromage blanc
60-140ml/2 fl oz-¼ pint milk
30g/1oz/1 cup watercress leaves, and
 thin stalks
30ml/2 tbsps chopped fresh herbs
Juice and grated rind of ½ lemon
Salt and pepper

Combine the beans, water and salt in a casserole dish and cover loosely. Cook on HIGH for 4 minutes, stirring once or twice. Leave to stand while preparing the sauce. Heat the milk for 3 minutes on HIGH. If using low fat soft cheese, use the greater quantity of milk. Combine with the remaining ingredients, except the lemon rind, in a food processor and work until well blended. Drain the beans and pour over the sauce. Sprinkle on the lemon rind, and toss just before serving.

Asparagus Tied with Fresh Herbs

PREPARATION TIME: 15 minutes

MICROWAVE COOKING TIME: 14 minutes

SERVES: 4 people

900g/2lb asparagus spears
8 sprigs of fresh thyme or marjoram or
 8 chives

SAUCE
3 egg yolks
180g/6oz/¾ cup butter
30ml/2 tbsps white wine
Squeeze of lemon juice

*5ml/1 tsp chopped thyme, marjoram or
    chives
Salt and pepper*

Trim the thick ends of the asparagus
and place the spears in a shallow
dish. Add 140ml/¼ pint/½ cup water
and cover the dish loosely. Cook on
HIGH for 10 minutes. Drain and
keep warm. In a small, deep bowl,
heat the wine and butter for 2
minutes on HIGH. Remove from the
oven and gradually beat in the egg
yolks. Cook on HIGH 10 seconds
and then stir. Repeat the process
until the sauce thickens, which takes
about 2 minutes. Add the lemon
juice, chopped herbs, salt and pepper.
Tie up 4 bundles of asparagus with
the chosen herbs. Serve the
asparagus with the sauce.

Broccoli with Toasted Sunflower Seeds

| **PREPARATION TIME:** 10 minutes |
| **MICROWAVE COOKING TIME:**
4½-5½ minutes |
| **SERVES:** 4 people |

*450g/1lb broccoli
30g/2 tbsps butter or margarine
120g/4oz/1 cup toasted, salted sunflower
    seeds
Pepper
5ml/1 tsp lemon juice (if desired)*

Trim the ends of the broccoli stalks
and separate into even-sized pieces.
Place in a large casserole or shallow
dish with 60ml/2 fl oz/¼ cup water.
Cover loosely and cook 4-5 minutes
on HIGH. Melt the butter for
30 seconds on HIGH, stir in the
sunflower seeds and add pepper and
lemon juice. Drain the broccoli and
sprinkle over the sunflower seeds to
serve.

Broccoli and Cauliflower Mold with Salsa

| **PREPARATION TIME:** 25 minutes |
| **MICROWAVE COOKING TIME:**
7½ minutes |

| **SERVES:** 4-6 people |

*1 small head cauliflower
225g/8oz broccoli*

DRESSING
*45ml/3 tbsps oil
15ml/1 tbsp wine vinegar
5ml/1 tsp ground mustard
½ clove garlic, minced
Salt and pepper*

SALSA
*4-5 tomatoes, depending on size
1 green pepper, chopped
15ml/1 tbsp oil
1 green chili pepper, finely chopped
5ml/1 tsp cumin seed or ground cumin
4 spring onions, finely chopped
Salt and pepper*

**This page: Broccoli and
Cauliflower Mold with Salsa.
Facing page: Broccoli with Toasted
Sunflower Seeds (top) and Brussels
Sprouts and Hazelnuts (bottom).**

Divide the cauliflower into flowerets
and trim down any long, thick stalks.
Trim the broccoli stalks to within
5cm/2 inches of the flowerets and
combine with the cauliflower in a
deep bowl. Add 30ml/2 tbsps water
and a pinch of salt. Cover loosely
and cook 3 minutes on HIGH. Mix
the dressing ingredients together
thoroughly. Drain the vegetables well
and pour the dressing over the
vegetables while still warm. Arrange
the vegetables in a deep 570ml/
1 pint/2 cup bowl, alternating the

2 vegetables. Press lightly to push the vegetables together. Leave the vegetables to cool in the bowl and then refrigerate. Put the tomatoes in a bowl of very hot water. Microwave 30 seconds on HIGH. Put the tomatoes into cold water and then peel and chop roughly. Heat the oil in a large bowl for 30 seconds on HIGH. Add the green pepper, chili pepper and cumin. Cook for 2 minutes on HIGH. Stir in the tomatoes, onions, salt and pepper and leave to cool. Turn out the vegetables carefully onto a serving plate and spoon the salsa around the base. Serve cold. Both the mold and the salsa may be prepared several hours in advance. If left overnight, the broccoli may discolour the cauliflower.

Vegetable Stir Fry with Tofu

PREPARATION TIME: 20 minutes

MICROWAVE COOKING TIME: 7½ minutes

SERVES: 4 people

60ml/2 fl oz/¼ cup oil
Blanched whole almonds
225g/8oz tofu
4 spears broccoli
120g/4oz peapods/mangetout
120g/4oz bean sprouts
120g/4oz baby corn-on-the-cob
1 red pepper, sliced
60g/2oz/½ cup water chestnuts, sliced
1 clove garlic, minced
140ml/¼ pint/½ cup vegetable stock
10ml/2 tsps cornstarch/cornflour
60ml/2 fl oz/4 tbsps soy sauce
Dash sherry
Dash sesame oil
Salt and pepper
4 spring onions/green onions, sliced

Heat a browning dish for 5 minutes on HIGH. Add the oil and fry the almonds for 5 minutes, stirring often to brown evenly. Remove the almonds from the dish and set them aside. Cut out the broccoli flowerets and reserve. Slice the stalks diagonally. If the corn cobs are large cut in half lengthwise. Cook the broccoli and the corn together for 1 minute on HIGH. Add the garlic, red pepper, peapods/mangetout, water chestnuts and the broccoli flowerets. Mix the soy sauce, sesame oil, sherry, stock, and cornstarch/cornflour together. Pour over the vegetables and cook 1 minute on HIGH. Add the bean sprouts, almonds, spring/green onions and the tofu, cut in small cubes. Cook 30 seconds on HIGH. Serve immediately.

Vegetables Mornay

PREPARATION TIME: 25 minutes

MICROWAVE COOKING TIME: 24-28 minutes

SERVES: 4-6 people

225g/8oz new potatoes, scrubbed but not peeled
125g/8oz button or pickling onions, peeled
15g/1 tbsp butter
Pinch sugar
2-3 carrots, cut in strips
2 parsnips, cut in strips
120g/4oz mangetout/peapods
120g/4oz button mushrooms
30g/2 tbsps butter
Salt

SAUCE
45g/3 tbsps butter
45g/3 tbsps flour
5ml/1 tsp dry mustard
Pinch cayenne pepper
570ml/1 pint/2 cups milk
120g/4oz/1 cup Cheddar cheese, shredded
Salt and pepper
Nutmeg

Cook the new potatoes in 60ml/ 2 fl oz/¼ cup water with a pinch of salt for 8-10 minutes on HIGH in a deep, covered dish. Leave to stand 5 minutes. Cook the carrots and parsnips together in 60ml/2 fl oz/ ¼ cup water in a covered dish for 6 minutes on HIGH. Combine the onions with the sugar and 15g/1 tbsp butter in a deep bowl. Cook, covered, for 7 minutes on HIGH. Stir twice while cooking. Melt the remaining butter for the vegetables and add the mangetout/peapods and mushrooms. Cook for 2 minutes on HIGH. Leave all the vegetables covered while preparing the sauce. Melt the butter for 1 minute on HIGH in a glass measure. Stir in the flour, mustard and cayenne pepper. Gradually whisk in the milk and add the salt and pepper. Cook for 3-4 minutes on HIGH, whisking after 1 minute, until the sauce has thickened and is bubbling. Stir in the cheese to melt. Arrange the vegetables on a serving dish, keeping each different vegetable in a separate pile. Coat with some of the sauce and sprinkle on nutmeg. Serve remaining sauce separately.

Brussels Sprouts and Hazelnuts

PREPARATION TIME: 20 minutes

MICROWAVE COOKING TIME: 20-21 minutes

SERVES: 4 people

60g/2oz/½ cup hazelnuts
450g/1lb Brussels sprouts
30g/2 tbsps butter or margarine
Salt and pepper

Put the nuts into a small, deep bowl. Cover with hot water and heat 3 minutes on HIGH. Leave to soak for 10 minutes. Drain and rub off the skins. Leave the nuts to dry. Heat a browning dish 5 minutes on HIGH and drop in the butter. Add the nuts and cook 5 minutes on HIGH, stirring every 30 seconds to brown the nuts evenly. Cook the Brussels sprouts with 30ml/2 tbsps water and a pinch of salt in a lightly covered bowl or a cooking bag. Cook for 7-8 minutes on HIGH or until tender. Drain and combine with the nuts and butter.

Facing page: Vegetable Stir Fry with Tofu.

Ginger Sesame Carrots

PREPARATION TIME: 10 minutes

MICROWAVE COOKING TIME:
7½-10½ minutes

SERVES: 4-6 people

900g/2lb carrots, sliced diagonally
30g/1oz/2 tbsps butter or margarine
30g/1oz/2 tbsps brown sugar
7.5ml/1½ tsps ground ginger or 1 small
*   piece fresh ginger, grated*
30g/1oz/¼ cup sesame seeds
Dash soy sauce
Dash sesame oil
Salt and pepper

Place the carrots in a casserole dish with 60ml/2 fl oz/¼ cup water. Add a pinch of salt, cover and cook on HIGH for 7-10 minutes. Leave to stand while melting the butter for 30 seconds on HIGH. Stir in the brown sugar, ginger, sesame seeds, sesame oil, soy sauce, salt and pepper. Add 15-30ml/1-2 tbsps of the cooking liquid from the carrots to the sesame-ginger mixture. Stir in the carrots to coat with the sauce.

Pommes Noisettes

PREPARATION TIME: 15 minutes plus overnight refrigeration

MICROWAVE COOKING TIME:
14-15 minutes

SERVES: 4-6 people

450g/1lb potatoes, scrubbed but not
*   peeled*
30ml/2 tbsps water
30g/1oz/2 tbsps butter
Salt and pepper
60g/2oz/½ cup grated Gruyère cheese
60g/2oz/½ cup ground browned
*   hazelnuts*
Chopped parsley

Prick the potato skins with a fork. Put the potatoes and water into a covered dish and cook 12 minutes on HIGH until tender. Drain the potatoes and cut in half. Scoop out the pulp and mash with a fork or potato masher. Beat in the butter, salt, pepper and cheese. Allow to cool and then refrigerate until cold.

Shape into 2.5cm/1 inch balls. Roll the potatoes in the nuts. Place in a circle on a baking sheet or serving dish and heat 2-3 minutes on HIGH. Sprinkle with chopped parsley before serving.

Dilled White Cabbage

PREPARATION TIME: 10 minutes

MICROWAVE COOKING TIME:
8 minutes plus 5 minutes standing time

SERVES: 4-6 people

**This page: Vegetable Mornay.
Facing page: Ginger Sesame Carrots
(top) and Pommes Noisettes
(bottom).**

1 medium head white cabbage or Dutch
*   cabbage, shredded*
30g/2 tbsps butter or margarine
Pinch sugar
30ml/2 tbsps dill seed
30ml/2 tbsps white wine vinegar
30ml/2 tbsps chopped fresh dill
Salt and pepper

Place the cabbage in a large casserole or bowl with 30ml/2 tbsps water and the remaining ingredients except the chopped fresh dill. Cover loosely and cook 8 minutes on HIGH, stirring twice. Leave to stand, covered, 5 minutes before serving. Sprinkle with the fresh dill.

Beets with Sour Cream and Dill

PREPARATION TIME: 20 minutes

MICROWAVE COOKING TIME: 13-17 minutes plus 10 minutes standing time

SERVES: 4 people

4-8 beetroot/beets, depending on size
280ml/½ pint/1 cup sour cream
2.5ml/1 tsp grated fresh horseradish
1 small bunch dill
Salt and pepper

Place raw beets, unpeeled, in 140-280ml/¼-½ pint/½-1 cup water depending on the number of beets. Use a casserole or a bowl covered with pierced cling film/plastic wrap. Cook 12-16 minutes. Leave to stand 10 minutes before peeling. If using pre-cooked beets, just peel them and heat through 1 minute on HIGH. Slice into 6mm/¼ inch slices. Arrange in a serving dish. Mix the sour cream, horseradish, dill, salt and pepper together. Spoon over the beets and heat through 30 seconds to 1 minute on HIGH. Do not allow the sour cream to boil. Garnish with a few sprigs of fresh dill and serve immediately.

Sweet and Sour Red Cabbage with Apple

PREPARATION TIME: 15 minutes

MICROWAVE COOKING TIME: 9-10 minutes plus 5 minutes standing time

SERVES: 4-6 people

30g/2 tbsps butter or margarine
1 medium head red cabbage, shredded
1 small onion, finely chopped

1 apple, cored and chopped
30g/2 tbsps brown sugar
30ml/2 tbsps red wine vinegar
140ml/¼ pint/½ cup water
Pinch cinnamon
Salt and pepper

GARNISH
15g/1 tbsp butter or margarine
1 apple, cored and chopped
Chopped parsley

Melt the butter or margarine in a deep casserole dish for 30 seconds on HIGH. Add all the remaining ingredients except the garnish and cover with pierced cling film/plastic wrap. Cook on HIGH for 8 minutes. Leave to stand, covered, 5 minutes while preparing the garnish. Melt the butter or margarine 30 seconds on HIGH in a small bowl. Add the apple and cook 1 minute on HIGH, uncovered, to partially soften. Toss with the parsley and sprinkle on top of the cabbage.

This page: Beets with Sour Cream and Dill. **Facing page:** Sweet and Sour Red Cabbage with Apple (top) and Dilled White Cabbage (bottom).

Creamed Spring/Green Onions

PREPARATION TIME: 10 minutes

MICROWAVE COOKING TIME: 5 minutes

SERVES: 4 people

2 bunches spring/green onions
15g/½ oz/1 tbsp butter or margarine
Salt and pepper
280ml/½ pint/1 cup low fat soft cheese
* or fromage blanc*
5ml/1 tsp chopped basil
5ml/1 tsp chopped parsley
140ml/¼ pint/½ cup milk

60g/2oz/½ cup chopped pine-nuts or
  walnuts
1.25ml/¼ tsp ground nutmeg
Squeeze lemon juice
Salt and pepper

GARNISH
Whole pine-nuts

ACCOMPANIMENTS
Lettuce
Buttered toast or rolls

Cook the spinach for 4 minutes on
HIGH in a loosely covered bowl.
Cook in the moisture that clings to
the leaves. Rinse under cold water,
drain very well and chop finely. Mix
with the cheese and milk and add the
garlic, nuts, nutmeg, lemon juice, salt
and pepper. Cut about 5cm/2 inches
off the tops of the peppers. Remove
the stems and chop the flesh finely.
Remove the cores and seeds from the
peppers. Place the whole and
chopped peppers into a large bowl or
casserole and cover with hot water.
Cook for 2-3 minutes on HIGH, and
rinse immediately under cold water.
Drain the whole peppers upside-
down on paper towels. Drain the
chopped peppers well and add to the
spinach pâté. Fill the drained pepper
cups with the spinach mixture.
Arrange on serving plates with the
lettuce leaves and top with whole
pine-nuts. Serve with hot buttered
toast or rolls.

Ratatouille

PREPARATION TIME: 35 minutes
MICROWAVE COOKING TIME: 14 minutes
SERVES: 4-6 people

30ml/2 tbsps oil
1 onion, sliced
1 aubergine/eggplant
2 courgettes/zucchini
1 green pepper
1 red pepper

**This page: Creamed Spring/Green
Onions (top) and Spinach with
Blue Cheese and Walnuts (bottom).
Facing page: Ratatouille.**

Wash the onions, barely remove the
root ends and trim off about 5cm/
2 inches off the green tops. Melt
butter in a casserole for 30 seconds
on HIGH. Add the onions, salt,
pepper and cover loosely with cling
film/plastic wrap. Cook 3 minutes
on HIGH. Remove the onions and
keep covered in a serving dish. Add
the cheese, herbs, milk, salt and
pepper to the casserole and stir
together well. Cook 1 minute on
HIGH. Add the onions and heat
through 30 seconds on HIGH. Serve
immediately.

Spinach and Ricotta Pâté in Red Pepper Cups

PREPARATION TIME: 20 minutes
MICROWAVE COOKING TIME: 6-8 minutes
SERVES: 4 people

4 medium-size sweet red peppers
900g/2lb fresh spinach, washed with
  stalks removed
450g/1lb ricotta, cottage or cream cheese
45ml/3 tbsps milk
1 small clove garlic, crushed

120g/4oz mushrooms, sliced
1 clove garlic, crushed
10ml/2 tsps chopped fresh basil
5ml/1 tsp chopped parsley
15ml/1 tbsp tomato purée/paste
1 bay leaf
30ml/2 tbsps white wine
Salt and pepper

Cut the aubergine/eggplant in half, score the flesh lightly and sprinkle with salt. Leave on paper towels for ½ hour to draw out any bitterness. Heat the oil in a casserole for 30 seconds on HIGH. Add the onion and garlic and cook 2 minutes on HIGH. Wash the aubergine/eggplant and dry it well. Slice it thinly and slice the courgettes/zucchini and peppers and add to the onions. Cook 5 minutes on HIGH, loosely covered. Add the herbs, bay leaf, tomato

purée/paste, wine, salt and pepper and cook a further 5 minutes on HIGH. Add the mushrooms and tomatoes and cook 2 minutes on HIGH. Remove the bay leaf before serving.

Spinach with Blue Cheese and Walnuts

PREPARATION TIME:	15 minutes
MICROWAVE COOKING TIME: 4½ minutes	
SERVES: 4-6 people	

900g/2lb fresh spinach, washed with
    stalks removed
30g/1oz/2 tbsps butter or margarine
Nutmeg
Salt and pepper

This page: Spinach and Ricotta Pâté in Red Pepper Cups. Facing page: Red Lentil and Mushroom Loaf.

120g/4oz/1 cup coarsely chopped
    walnuts
120g/4oz/1 cup crumbled blue cheese

Place spinach in a large bowl with a pinch of salt. Cover the bowl loosely and cook in the water that clings to the leaves. Microwave on HIGH for 4 minutes. Press between 2 plates to drain thoroughly. Melt the butter in a serving dish for 30 seconds on HIGH. Add the spinach, pepper, nutmeg, walnuts and cheese and toss together to serve.

RECIPES WITH PULSES

Red Lentil and Mushroom Loaf

PREPARATION TIME: 20 minutes

MICROWAVE COOKING TIME:
25-28 minutes plus the indicated standing times

SERVES: 4-6 people

180g/6oz/1 cup red lentils, picked over and washed
340ml/12oz/1½ cups vegetable stock or water
1 clove garlic, finely chopped
15ml/1 tbsp chopped parsley
15ml/1 tbsp chopped tarragon
90g/3oz mushrooms, coarsely chopped
120g/4oz/½ cup cream cheese
1 egg plus 30ml/2 tbsps heavy/double cream
Salt and pepper

QUICK TOMATO SAUCE
1 400g/14oz can tomatoes
15ml/1 tbsp tomato purée/paste
5ml/1 tsp dry tarragon
Pinch sugar
Salt and pepper
15ml/1 tbsp chopped fresh tarragon

Cover the lentils with water and leave to stand overnight or microwave 10 minutes to boil the water. Allow the lentils to boil 2 minutes further on HIGH. Allow to stand 1 hour. Combine the lentils with stock or fresh water in a large bowl. Partially cover the bowl and cook 10-12 minutes on HIGH or until the lentils are very soft. Check the amount of liquid and add more if necessary as the lentils cook. Allow to stand for 5 minutes. Mash to a thick purée. Beat the eggs and cream together and add to the purée. Stir in the remaining ingredients and press into a lightly greased loaf dish. Cover with cling film/plastic wrap pierced several times. Cook on MEDIUM for 7-8 minutes until firm around the edges but soft in the middle. Leave to stand 5-10 minutes to firm. May be served hot with the sauce or cold. To prepare the sauce combine all the ingredients except the fresh tarragon. Cook, uncovered, 8 minutes or until thickened. Purée in a food processor and strain to remove the seeds if desired. Add the chopped fresh tarragon and serve with the red lentil and mushroom loaf.

Beans Bourguignonne

PREPARATION TIME: 20 minutes

MICROWAVE COOKING TIME:
1 hour 43 minutes plus indicated
standing times

SERVES: 4 people

*225g/8oz/2 cups field beans (other dark
  coloured beans may be substituted)*
45ml/3 tbsps oil
4 carrots
*225g/8oz small onions, peeled and left
  whole*
225g/8oz mushrooms, quartered
140ml/¼ pint/½ cup vegetable stock
280ml/½ pint/1 cup red wine
1 bay leaf
5ml/1 tsp chopped thyme
10ml/2 tsps chopped parsley
45g/3 tbsps butter or margarine
*4 slices wholemeal/whole-wheat bread,
  crusts removed*

Cover the beans with water and
leave to stand overnight or
microwave for 10 minutes on HIGH
to bring to the boil. Allow the beans
to boil for 2 minutes. Leave to stand
for 1 hour before using. Cover with
fresh water and add the bay leaf and
a pinch of salt. Loosely cover the
dish and cook on MEDIUM for
45 minutes. Leave to stand for
10 minutes before draining. Heat a
browning dish for 5 minutes on
HIGH. Pour in the oil and add the
carrots, onions and mushrooms.
Cook on HIGH for 2 minutes,
stirring frequently to brown slightly.
Remove the vegetables from the
browning dish and add 45g/3 tbsps
butter or margarine. Heat the butter
for 1 minute on HIGH and put in the
bread, cut into triangles. Brown the
croutes 1 minute on HIGH and turn
over. Brown the other side for
1 minute on HIGH and drain on
paper towels. Put the beans into a
casserole with the vegetable stock
and the red wine. Cover the
casserole and cook an additional
15 minutes on HIGH or until the
beans are almost tender. Add the
carrots, onions, mushrooms, thyme,
parsley and additional salt and
pepper. Re-cover the casserole and
cook a further 15-20 minutes on
HIGH or until the vegetables and the

beans are completely tender. Leave to
stand for 15 minutes before serving.
Re-heat the bread for 1 minute on
MEDIUM. Remove the bay leaf and
the beans and transfer them to a
serving dish and surround with the
croutes to serve.

Red Beans Creole

PREPARATION TIME: 20 minutes

MICROWAVE COOKING TIME:
1 hour 23 minutes plus standing
times indicated in the recipe

SERVES: 4 people

180g/6oz/1 cup red kidney beans
180g/6oz/1½ cups long-grain rice
30g/2 tbsps butter or margarine
1 green pepper, cut in strips
*3-4 tomatoes, peeled, seeded and cut in
  strips*

**This page: Red Beans Creole.
Facing page: Chickpea and Pepper
Casserole (top) and Beans
Bourguignonne (bottom).**

120g/4oz mushrooms, sliced
4 spring/green onions, chopped
30ml/2 tbsps chopped parsley
Cayenne pepper
Ground nutmeg
1 bay leaf
Salt and pepper

Cover the beans with water and
leave overnight, or microwave 10
minutes to boil the water. Allow the
beans to boil for 2 minutes. Leave to
stand 1 hour. Cover with fresh water
and add a pinch of salt and the bay
leaf. Cook on MEDIUM for 55
minutes to 1 hour. Allow to stand
10 minutes before draining. The
beans must be completely cooked.

Save the cooking liquid to use as stock in other recipes if desired. Place rice in a large bowl or casserole dish, add 570ml/1 pint/2 cups water and a pinch of salt. Cook about 10 minutes on HIGH. Leave to stand for 5 minutes before draining. Heat the butter or margarine 30 seconds on HIGH in a casserole dish, and add the pepper strips and mushrooms. Cook for 2 minutes, stirring once. Stir in the cayenne pepper, nutmeg, salt, pepper, rice and beans. Cook 1 minute on HIGH. Add the spring/green onions, parsley and tomatoes and cook a further 30 seconds on HIGH.

Chickpea and Pepper Casserole

PREPARATION TIME: 20 minutes

MICROWAVE COOKING TIME:
51 minutes to 1 hour 6 minutes

SERVES: 4 people

225g/8oz/1⅓ cups chickpeas (garbanzo beans)
30ml/2 tbsps oil
1 large onion, sliced
1 green pepper, sliced
1 red pepper, sliced
1 clove garlic, minced
10ml/2 tsps chopped parsley
5ml/1 tsp chopped mint
2.5ml/½ tsp ground cumin
Salt and pepper
4 tomatoes, seeded and cut in strips

ACCOMPANIMENT
1 cucumber, thinly sliced
280ml/½ pint/1 cup yogurt
Salt and pepper

Leave the chickpeas to soak in water overnight or use the microwave rehydrating method. Cover with fresh water and add a pinch of salt. Cover the bowl and cook 45 minutes to 1 hour until tender. Drain and reserve the liquid. Heat the oil 30 seconds on HIGH. Add the onion, peppers, garlic and cumin. Cook 1 minute on HIGH. Add the chickpeas and half the cooking liquid. Cook a further 5 minutes on HIGH. Add parsley, mint, tomatoes, and

season with salt and pepper. Cook 30 seconds on HIGH. Combine the accompaniment ingredients and serve with the casserole.

Vegetable Cassoulet

PREPARATION TIME: 20 minutes

MICROWAVE COOKING TIME:
1 hour 40 minutes plus indicated standing times

SERVES: 4 people

225g/8oz/2 cups haricot/navy beans
60ml/2 fl oz/¼ cup oil
2 cloves garlic, minced
2 small leeks, cut in 2.5cm/1 inch pieces
3 carrots, cut in 2.5cm/1 inch chunks
4 sticks celery, cut in 2.5cm/1 inch pieces
2 parsnips, halved, cored and cut in 2.5cm/1 inch pieces
2 turnips, peeled and cut in 2.5cm/1 inch pieces
120g/4oz mushrooms, quartered
15ml/1 tbsp Worcestershire sauce
1 bay leaf
15ml/1 tbsp marjoram, chopped
430ml/¾ pint/1½ cups vegetable stock
Salt and pepper

TOPPING
30g/2 tbsps butter or margarine
60g/2oz/½ cup dry breadcrumbs

Heat a browning dish for 5 minutes on HIGH. Melt the butter for the topping and add the crumbs. Stirring frequently, cook on HIGH for 2-3 minutes until the crumbs are golden brown and crisp. Set them aside. Add the oil to the browning dish and heat for 1 minute on HIGH. Add all of the vegetables and cook 2 minutes on HIGH to brown. Stir frequently. Remove the vegetables from the browning dish and de-glaze the dish with the vegetable stock. Stir to remove any sediment from browning the vegetables. Cover the beans with water and leave to soak overnight or microwave for 10 minutes to bring the water to the boil. Allow the beans to boil for 2 minutes. Leave them to stand for 1 hour. Drain the beans and put them into the casserole dish with the garlic, bay leaf, Worcestershire sauce, marjoram,

salt and pepper. Add half the stock, cover and cook for 1 hour on HIGH. Add more stock as necessary during cooking. The mixture should be fairly thick at the end of the cooking time. Add the vegetables and re-cover the dish. Cook an additional 15-20 minutes on HIGH, adding more stock if necessary. When the beans are tender and most of the liquid has been absorbed, sprinkle on the brown crumbs and cook for 5 minutes on HIGH. Leave the cassoulet to stand for 15 minutes before serving. The cassoulet may be prepared in advance and refrigerated. Re-heat 2-3 minutes on HIGH. Add the crumbs and cook a further 5 minutes on HIGH before serving.

Chinese Black Bean Casserole

PREPARATION TIME: 20 minutes

MICROWAVE COOKING TIME:
1 hour 33 minutes plus indicated standing time

SERVES: 4 people

450g/1lb black beans
1 small piece fresh ginger root, grated
1 clove garlic, minced
10ml/2 tsps 5-spice powder
1 piece star anise
6-8 sticks celery
1 small can water chestnuts, drained and sliced
90ml/3 fl oz/⅓ cup sherry
15ml/1 tbsp soy sauce
5ml/1 tsp sesame seed oil

GARNISH
120g/4oz bean sprouts
4 spring/green onions shredded

Cover the beans with water and leave to stand overnight, or microwave on HIGH for 10 minutes to boil the water. Allow the beans to boil for 2 minutes and leave to stand for 1 hour before using. If using salted

Facing page: Chinese Black Bean Casserole (top) and Vegetable Cassoulet (bottom).

Chinese black beans, soak in cold water for ½ hour and drain. Cut the cooking time in half. Cover the beans with water and add the grated ginger, star anise, 5-spice powder and garlic. Add a pinch of salt and pepper and loosely cover the bowl. Cook for 1 hour on HIGH, stirring occasionally. Add the celery and cook a further 15 minutes on HIGH. Add the sherry, soy sauce and sesame oil and cook a further 5 minutes on HIGH. If a lot of liquid remains, continue to cook until the liquid is absorbed. Add the water chestnuts just before serving and cook 1 minute on HIGH to heat through. Garnish with the bean sprouts and shredded spring/green onion to serve.

Butter Bean, Lemon and Fennel Salad

PREPARATION TIME: 15 minutes

MICROWAVE COOKING TIME:
1 hour 12 minutes plus standing times indicated in the recipe

SERVES: 4 people

225g/8oz/2 cups butter beans
1 large bulb Florentine fennel, thinly sliced
Juice and rind of 1 lemon
60ml/4 tbsps oil
Pinch sugar
Salt and pepper

Cover the beans with water and leave overnight, or microwave 10 minutes to boil the water and allow the beans to boil for 2 minutes. Leave to stand for 1 hour. Cover with fresh water and add a pinch of salt. Cook on MEDIUM for 55 minutes to 1 hour. The beans must be cooked all the way through. Allow to stand for 10 minutes before draining. Boil 570ml/1 pint/2 cups water for 10 minutes on HIGH. Reserve the green tops of the fennel and blanch the sliced bulb in the water for 2 minutes on HIGH. Drain thoroughly. Pare the rind from the lemon and scrape off any white pith. Cut the rind into very thin strips and squeeze the juice from the lemon. Mix with the oil, pinch sugar, salt and

pepper. Chop the fennel tops and add to the dressing. Pour over the drained beans and fennel slices. Toss to coat thoroughly. Serve on a bed of lettuce or radicchio.

Black-Eyed Bean/Pea and Orange Salad

PREPARATION TIME: 20 minutes

MICROWAVE COOKING TIME:
1 hour plus 10 minutes standing time

SERVES: 4 people

225g/8oz/1½ cups black-eyed beans/ peas
1 bay leaf
1 slice onion
Salt

SALAD
4 oranges
Small handful fresh basil leaves
30ml/2 tbsps chopped parsley
6 black olives, pitted
1 large bunch watercress

DRESSING
Juice and rind of 1 orange
75ml/5 tbsps oil
4 spring/green onions, chopped
Salt and pepper

Cover the beans with water and leave overnight, or microwave for 10 minutes to boil the water. Allow the beans to boil for 2 minutes. Leave to stand for 1 hour. Cover with fresh water and add a pinch of salt, the bay leaf and the slice of onion. Cook on MEDIUM for 55 minutes to 1 hour. Allow to stand 10 minutes before draining. Mix the oil and the juice and grated rind of 1 orange with the basil leaves, chopped, chopped parsley, chopped spring/green onions and salt and pepper. Pour the dressing over the beans and add the black olives, sliced, and toss. Peel and segment the remaining four oranges. Chop the segments of two of the oranges and add those to the bean salad. Arrange the watercress on 4 individual plates and pile on the bean salad. Arrange the remaining orange segments on the plates and serve immediately.

Curried Lentils

PREPARATION TIME: 25 minutes

MICROWAVE COOKING TIME: 36 minutes plus 5-10 minutes standing time

SERVES: 4 people

225g/8oz lentils, brown or green
60g/2oz/¼ cup butter or margarine
1 large onion, chopped
1 clove garlic, chopped
1 red or green chili pepper, finely chopped
5ml/1 tsp cumin
5ml/1 tsp coriander
5ml/1 tsp turmeric
2.5ml/½ tsp cinnamon
2.5ml/½ tsp nutmeg
60g/2oz/½ cup whole blanched almonds
570ml/1 pint/2 cups vegetable stock
Salt and pepper
Desiccated coconut
Coriander leaves

APPLE AND CUCUMBER RELISH
2 apples, cored and chopped
60g/2oz/½ cup raisins
120g/4oz/1 cup chopped cucumber
60ml/2 fl oz/¼ cup mango chutney

SPICED BANANAS
2 bananas, sliced
30g/2 tbsps butter or margarine
Pinch nutmeg
Pinch cinnamon
15ml/1 tbsp brown sugar
15ml/1 tbsp lemon juice
Garam masala

TOMATO AND ONION RELISH
2 tomatoes, chopped
1 green pepper, chopped

1 small onion, chopped
Juice of ½ lemon
10ml/2 tsps oil
Pinch cayenne pepper
Salt

Cover the lentils with water and leave to soak overnight. Alternatively microwave 10 minutes to boil the water and allow the lentils to boil 2 minutes. Leave to stand for 1 hour. Melt the butter for 1 minute on HIGH in a large casserole dish. Add the onion, garlic, chili pepper and spices. Cook 4 minutes on MEDIUM. Drain the lentils and add to the casserole with the vegetable stock. Cover and cook on HIGH for 30 minutes until the lentils are tender. Allow to stand 5-10 minutes before serving. Heat a browning dish for 5 minutes on HIGH. Melt the

Facing page: Butter Bean, Lemon and Fennel Salad (top) and Black-Eyed Bean/Pea and Orange Salad (bottom). This page: Curried Lentils.

butter and add the sliced bananas. Cook 30 seconds on HIGH on one side and turn over. Cook a further 30 seconds and sprinkle with the spices and the lemon juice. Sprinkle with garam masala just before serving. Combine the ingredients for the apple and cucumber relish and those for the tomato and onion relish and serve the accompaniments with the curried lentils. Sprinkle the lentils with desiccated coconut and garnish with coriander leaves before serving.

Microwave
VEGETARIAN
MAIN COURSES

Curried Vegetables

PREPARATION TIME: 20 minutes

MICROWAVE COOKING TIME: 17 minutes

SERVES: 4 people

2 medium-size potatoes, peeled and cut
  into 2.5cm/1 inch chunks
3 carrots, cut into 2.5cm/1 inch chunks
3 courgettes/zucchini, sliced
120g/4oz okra, stems trimmed
60g/2oz mushrooms, quartered
2 tomatoes, quartered
1 large onion, sliced
45ml/3 tbsps oil
1 clove garlic, minced
1 red or green chili pepper, minced after
  removing the seeds
30ml/2 tbsps flour
5ml/1 tsp ground cumin
5ml/1 tsp ground coriander
5ml/1 tsp turmeric
10ml/2 tsps mustard seed
2.5ml/½ tsp paprika
Pinch ground cloves
Bay leaf
570ml/1 pint/2 cups vegetable stock or
  vegetable cooking liquid and water
140ml/¼ pint/½ cup natural yogurt
Salt and pepper

GARNISH
Chopped coriander leaves

Cook the potatoes and carrots
together in a large, covered casserole.
Add just enough salted water to
cover the vegetables. Cook on HIGH
for 8 minutes. Add the courgettes/
zucchini and okra after 6 minutes
cooking. Leave the vegetables to
stand, covered, for 5 minutes.
Reserve the quartered tomatoes and
mushrooms. Heat the oil for 1 minute
on HIGH and add the onion, garlic,
chili pepper and mushrooms. Cook

for 1 minute on HIGH. Stir in the
flour and spices and cook a further
1 minute on HIGH. Add the liquid
gradually, stirring until smooth. Add
the bay leaf, salt and pepper and
cook 5 minutes on HIGH, stirring
frequently after 1 minute. When
thickened, remove the bay leaf and
add the cooked vegetables and the
quartered tomatoes. Heat through
1 minute on HIGH. Serve with rice
and chutney. The accompaniments
from the Curried Lentil recipe may
also be served.

**This page: Pasta, Peas and Peppers.
Facing page: Gratin of Vegetable
Oliver (top) and Curried Vegetables
(bottom).**

Pasta, Peas and Peppers

PREPARATION TIME: 20 minutes

MICROWAVE COOKING TIME:
10 minutes plus 10 minutes
standing time

SERVES: 4 people

225g/8oz/3 cups plain and whole-wheat
   pasta shells, mixed
225g/8oz/1 cup frozen peas
1 green pepper, shredded
1 yellow pepper, shredded
1 red pepper, shredded
4 spring/green onions, shredded
120g/4oz grated Parmesan cheese

DRESSING
140ml/¼ pint/½ cup oil
60ml/2 fl oz/¼ cup white wine vinegar
15ml/1 tbsp Dijon mustard
10ml/2 tsps poppy seeds
10ml/2 tsps chopped parsley
5ml/1 tsp chopped thyme
Salt and pepper

Cook the pasta 6 minutes in a large
bowl with 570ml/1 pint/2 cups
salted water. Leave to stand, covered,
10 minutes before draining. Cook the
peas and peppers in 30ml/2 tbsps
water for 2 minutes. Drain and allow
to cool, uncovered. Mix the dressing
ingredients together until well
blended. Pour over the pasta, add the
cheese and toss to coat the pasta
well. Add the peas, peppers and
spring/green onions and toss again to
mix all the ingredients before serving.

Pasta-Stuffed Cabbage Leaves

PREPARATION TIME: 20 minutes

MICROWAVE COOKING TIME:
29 minutes plus 10 minutes
standing time

SERVES: 4 people

1 head cabbage, white or green

FILLING
120g/4oz/¾ cup soup pasta
1 hard boiled egg, finely chopped
60g/2oz/½ cup walnuts, roughly
   chopped
15ml/1 tbsp chopped chives
30ml/2 tbsps chopped parsley
5ml/1 tsp chopped marjoram
Salt and pepper

SAUCE
1 450g/1lb can tomatoes
15ml/1 tbsp oil
120g/4oz mushrooms, sliced

1 small onion, diced
1 green pepper, diced
30ml/2 tbsps tomato purée/paste
1 bay leaf
Pinch sugar
Salt and pepper

Place the pasta in a large bowl with
570ml/1 pint/2 cups salted water
and cook for 5 minutes on HIGH.
Leave to stand, covered, 10 minutes
before draining. Put the cabbage
leaves in a large bowl or roasting bag
with 30ml/1 fl oz/2 tbsps water with
a pinch of salt. Cook 3-4 minutes on
HIGH. Lay flat on paper towels to
drain. Heat the oil for 30 seconds on
HIGH. Add the onions and peppers
for the sauce and cook 1 minute on
HIGH. Add the remaining sauce
ingredients and cook 8 minutes on
HIGH. Combine the drained pasta
with the remaining filling ingredients
and spoon on to the cabbage leaves.
Roll up the leaves, tucking in the
ends, and lay them in a serving dish.
Pour over the sauce and cook on
MEDIUM for 8 minutes. Serve
immediately.

Gratin of Vegetables Oliver

PREPARATION TIME: 20 minutes

MICROWAVE COOKING TIME:
12-13 minutes

SERVES: 4 people

TOPPING
120g/4oz/½ cup butter or margarine
   melted
225g/8oz/1 cup chopped, pitted black
   olives
120g/4oz/1 cup dry breadcrumbs
180g/6oz/1½ cups shredded Cheddar
   cheese
120g/4oz/1 cup chopped walnuts
10ml/2 tsps chopped fresh basil
Pinch cayenne pepper

VEGETABLES
4 courgettes/zucchini, sliced
1 bunch broccoli
4 carrots, sliced
225g/8oz French/green beans
2 red peppers, sliced
8 spring/green onions, sliced
Salt and pepper

Melt the butter for the topping for
30 seconds on HIGH. Stir in the
remaining ingredients and set aside.
Cook the carrots in 60ml/4 tbsps
water with a pinch of salt for 8
minutes. After 5 minutes add the
courgettes/zucchini, broccoli and
beans. Add the peppers and spring/
green onions 1 minute before the end
of cooking time. Drain the vegetables
and arrange in a serving dish.
Sprinkle lightly with salt and pepper
and sprinkle over the topping
ingredients. Bake 4 minutes on
MEDIUM or 5 minutes on a
combination setting in a microwave
convection oven. Serve immediately.

Watercress-Stuffed Potatoes

PREPARATION TIME: 25 minutes

MICROWAVE COOKING TIME:
27-29 minutes plus 5 minutes
standing time

SERVES: 4 people

4 large baking potatoes
140ml/¼ pint/½ cup milk
120g/4oz mushrooms, sliced
1 shallot, chopped
15g/1 tbsp butter or margarine
4 eggs
1 bunch watercress

SAUCE
45g/1½ oz/3 tbsps butter or margarine
30g/1oz/2 tbsps flour
Pinch dry mustard
Pinch cayenne pepper
280ml/½ pint/1 cup milk
60g/2oz/½ cup grated cheese
Salt and pepper

GARNISH
30g/1oz/¼ cup grated cheese
Reserved watercress

Wash and prick the potato skins
several times with a fork. Bake the
potatoes 10-12 minutes on HIGH.
Wrap them in foil and leave to stand
5 minutes. Pour 1150ml/2 pints/
4 cups hot water into a large, shallow
dish. Add 15ml/1 tbsp vinegar and
5ml/1 tsp salt. Heat the water 5
minutes on HIGH or until boiling.

reserving 4 sprigs for garnish. Add the chopped watercress to the potatoes and beat in the hot milk. Add salt and pepper to taste and pipe or spoon the potatoes on top of the cheese sauce in the potato shells. Sprinkle on cheese and cook for 3 minutes on HIGH to heat through and melt the cheese. Alternatively, heat 5 minutes on a combination setting in a microwave convection oven. Garnish with the watercress and serve immediately.

Mushroom Croquettes with Green Peppercorn Sauce

PREPARATION TIME: 25 minutes	
MICROWAVE COOKING TIME: 16-17 minutes	
SERVES: 4 people	

120g/4oz/1 cup finely chopped mushrooms
90g/3oz/1¾ cups fresh breadcrumbs
30g/1oz/2 tbsps butter or margarine
1 shallot, finely chopped
30g/1oz/2 tbsps flour
140ml/¼ pint/½ cup milk
5ml/1 tsp chopped parsley
5ml/1 tsp chopped thyme
1 beaten egg
Salt and pepper

COATING
Remaining beaten egg
Dry breadcrumbs
30-60ml/2-4 tbsps oil for frying

SAUCE
15g/1 tbsp butter or margarine
1 shallot, finely chopped
15g/1 tbsp flour
30ml/2 tbsps vermouth or white wine
280ml/½ pint/1 cup heavy/double cream
30ml/2 tbsps green peppercorns, drained and rinsed
1 small cap pimento, diced
Salt and pepper

Melt the butter for the croquettes for 1 minute on HIGH. Add the shallot and the mushrooms and cook 30

Break the eggs into a cup and slide them, one at a time into the water. Prick the yolks once with a sharp knife or skewer. Cook on MEDIUM for 3 minutes. Remove from the dish and place in enough cold water to cover them. Melt the 15g/1 tbsp butter in a small bowl for 30 seconds on HIGH. Add the mushrooms and shallot. Cook for 1 minute on HIGH and set aside. Melt the butter for the sauce for 30 seconds on HIGH in a glass measure. Add the flour, mustard, and cayenne pepper. Stir in the milk gradually and cook 3

This page: Pasta-Stuffed Cabbage Leaves (top) and Watercress-Stuffed Potatoes (bottom).

minutes on HIGH. Stir after 1 minute. Add the cheese and stir to melt. Cut a slice off the top of each potato and scoop out the pulp, leaving a border inside the skin. Fill with the mushrooms and top with one of the drained eggs. Spoon over the cheese sauce. Mash the potato and heat the milk for 2 minutes on HIGH. Chop the watercress leaves and thin stalks in a food processor,

1 shallot, finely chopped
30g/1oz/2 tbsps flour
140ml/¼ pint/½ cup milk
5ml/1 tsp chopped parsley
5ml/1 tsp chopped thyme
1 beaten egg
Salt and pepper

COATING
Beaten egg
Dry breadcrumbs
30-60ml/2-4 tbsps oil for frying

SAUCE
280ml/½ pint/1 cup heavy/double
 cream
15ml/1 tbsp pear brandy
60g/2oz/½ cup grated Parmesan cheese
Coarsely ground black pepper
Salt

GARNISH
4 small, ripe, unpeeled pears, halved and
 cored
Lemon juice
8 fresh sage leaves

Melt the butter for the escalopes for
1 minute on HIGH. Add the shallot
and cook 30 seconds on HIGH. Stir
in the flour and add the milk
gradually. Cook for 2 minutes on
HIGH until thickened. Add the
remaining escalope ingredients and
half the beaten egg. Spread the
mixture into a square pan and chill
until firm. Cut the mixture into
8 equal pieces and flatten into thin
patties. Coat with the remaining egg
and dry breadcrumbs, shaking off the
excess. If the patties become difficult
to handle, chill for 10 minutes in the
refrigerator before coating with egg
and crumbs. Heat a browning dish
for 5 minutes on HIGH and pour in
the oil. Heat for 30 seconds on
HIGH, put in the escalopes and
cover the dish. Cook for 2-3 minutes
on HIGH, turning over halfway
through the cooking time. Drain the
escalopes on paper towels. Boil the
cream and brandy for 6 minutes on
HIGH in a glass measure. Stir in the

seconds on HIGH. Stir in the flour
and add the milk gradually. Cook for
2 minutes on HIGH until thickened.
Add the remaining croquette
ingredients and half the beaten egg.
Spread the mixture into a square pan
and chill until firm. Cut the mixture
into 16 equal pieces and shape into
small ovals. Coat with the remaining
egg and press on the dry crumbs,
shaking off the excess. Heat a
browning dish for 5 minutes on
HIGH and pour in the oil. Heat for
30 seconds on HIGH and put in the
croquettes. Cover and cook 3-4
minutes on HIGH, turning over after
2 minutes. Drain on paper towels.
Heat the butter for the sauce for
30 seconds on HIGH in a small, deep
bowl. Add the shallot, finely
chopped and cook for 30 seconds on
HIGH. Stir in the flour, vermouth or
white wine and the cream. Season

lightly with salt and pepper and cook
for 3-4 minutes on HIGH, stirring
frequently. Add the green
peppercorns and the pimento
1 minute before the end of cooking
time. Arrange the croquettes in a
serving dish and pour over the sauce
to serve.

Hazelnut Escalopes with Pear Brandy Cream Sauce

PREPARATION TIME: 25 minutes
MICROWAVE COOKING TIME: 17-18 minutes
SERVES: 4 people

120g/4oz/1 cup ground hazelnuts
60g/2oz/1⅓ cups fresh breadcrumbs
30g/1oz/2 tbsps butter or margarine

**This page: Walnut Cutlets with
Three Pepper Salpicon. Facing
page: Mushroom Croquettes with
Green Peppercorn Sauce (top) and
Hazelnut Escalopes with Pear
Brandy Cream Sauce (bottom).**

cheese and pepper. Taste and add salt if desired. Heat for 30 seconds on HIGH to melt the cheese. Place a spoonful of the sauce on each of 4 serving plates. Brush the cut sides of the pears with lemon juice and arrange on the plates with the sage leaves. Place on the cutlets and spoon over some of the sauce to serve. Hand the rest of the sauce separately.

Walnut Cutlets with Three Pepper Salpicon

PREPARATION TIME: 25 minutes

MICROWAVE COOKING TIME: 17-18 minutes

SERVES: 4 people

CUTLETS
120g/4oz/1 cup walnuts, ground
60g/2oz/1⅓ cups fresh breadcrumbs
5ml/1 tsp chopped parsley
5ml/1 tsp chopped thyme
30g/1oz/2 tbsps butter or margarine
1 shallot, finely chopped
30g/1oz/2 tbsps flour
140ml/¼ pint/½ cup milk
1 beaten egg
Salt and pepper

COATING
Remaining beaten egg
Dry breadcrumbs
30-60ml/2-4 tbsps oil for frying

SALPICON
30g/1oz/2 tbsps butter or margarine
1 small onion, thinly sliced
15g/1 tbsp flour
Juice of 1 lemon
90ml/3oz/⅓ cup vegetable stock
1-2 green peppers, sliced
1-2 red peppers, sliced
1-2 yellow peppers, sliced
Pinch cayenne pepper
10ml/2 tsps capers
Salt and pepper

Melt the butter for the cutlets for 1 minute on HIGH. Add the shallot and cook 30 seconds on HIGH. Stir in the flour and add the milk gradually. Cook for 2 minutes on HIGH until thickened. Add the remaining cutlet ingredients and half the beaten egg. Spread the mixture

into a square pan and chill until firm. Cut the mixture into 8 equal portions and shape into cutlets or patties. Coat with the remaining egg and the dry breadcrumbs, shaking off the excess. Heat a browning dish for 5 minutes on HIGH. Pour in the oil and heat 30 seconds on HIGH. Put in the cutlets, cover the dish and cook 3-4 minutes on HIGH, turning over after 2 minutes. Drain on paper towels. Heat the butter for the salpicon 30 seconds on HIGH in a casserole. Add the onion and cook for 1 minute on HIGH. Stir in the flour and add the lemon juice and stock and cook for 1 minute on HIGH until very thick. Add the peppers and capers and cook a further 3 minutes on HIGH. Add the cayenne pepper, salt and pepper and serve with the cutlets.

Pasta Primavera

PREPARATION TIME: 20 minutes

MICROWAVE COOKING TIME: 14 minutes plus 10 minutes standing time

SERVES: 4 people

450g/1lb/6 cups pasta shapes, or noodles
225g/8oz asparagus
120g/4oz French/green beans
60g/2oz mushrooms, sliced
2 carrots
3 tomatoes peeled, seeded and cut in strips
6 spring/green onions
30ml/2 tbsps chopped parsley
10ml/2 tsps chopped tarragon
140ml/¼ pint/½ cup heavy/double cream
Salt and pepper

Cook the pasta 6 minutes on HIGH in 1150ml/2 pints/4 cups hot water with a pinch of salt and 15ml/1 tbsp oil. Cover and leave to stand 10 minutes before draining. Leave to drain completely. Slice the asparagus diagonally, leaving the tips whole. Cut the beans and carrots diagonally into thin slices. Cook the carrots and asparagus in 30ml/2 tbsps water for 4 minutes on HIGH, loosely covered. Add the beans and mushrooms and cook an additional 2 minutes on HIGH. Add to the drained pasta and stir in the cream, salt and pepper. Cook 1 minute on HIGH to heat the pasta. Add the tomatoes, onions, herbs and toss gently. Cook an additional 1 minute on HIGH. Serve immediately with grated cheese if desired.

Aubergine/Eggplant Rolls

PREPARATION TIME: 25 minutes

MICROWAVE COOKING TIME: 20-23 minutes

SERVES: 4 people

2-3 aubergines/eggplants, depending on
    size, sliced 1.25cm/½ inch thick
45ml/3 tbsps oil, or more as needed, for
    frying
120g/4oz/1 cup grated mozzarella cheese

SAUCE
1 450g/1lb can plum tomatoes
30ml/2 tbsps tomato purée/paste
1 onion, finely chopped
Pinch sugar
Pinch oregano
1 bay leaf
2 parsley stalks
Salt and pepper

FILLING
225g/8oz ricotta cheese
120g/4oz pitted black olives, chopped
60g/2oz/¼ cup grated Parmesan cheese
60g/2oz/¼ cup pine-nuts
15ml/1 tbsp white wine
1 clove garlic, finely minced
5ml/1 tsp each chopped parsley and basil
Pinch nutmeg
Salt and pepper

Facing page: Pasta Primavera. This page: Aubergine/Eggplant Rolls.

Lightly score the slices of aubergine/eggplant on both sides and sprinkle with salt. Leave on paper towels to stand for 30 minutes to draw out any bitterness. Combine all the sauce ingredients in a small, deep bowl. Cook, uncovered, for 8 minutes on HIGH. Remove the bay leaf and parsley stalks and purée in a food processor. Strain to remove the seeds if desired. Rinse the aubergine/eggplant and pat dry. Heat a browning dish for 5 minutes on HIGH. Pour in the oil and heat for 1 minute on HIGH. Add the aubergine/eggplant slices and brown for 1 minute per side. Cook in 2 or 3 batches if necessary and add more oil if needed. Drain on paper towels. Mix the filling ingredients and fill half of each aubergine/eggplant slice. Fill the bottom of a large, shallow baking dish with half the sauce. Fold the aubergine/eggplant slices in half and place on top of the sauce. Spoon over the remaining sauce, cover the dish loosely with cling film/plastic wrap and cook 3 minutes on HIGH. Sprinkle on the cheese and cook, uncovered, a further 2-3 minutes on MEDIUM. Alternatively, coat with sauce and sprinkle on the cheese and cook for 8 minutes on a combination setting of a microwave convection oven.

Vegetable Moussaka

PREPARATION TIME: 55 minutes

MICROWAVE COOKING TIME: 29 minutes

SERVES: 4 people

2 potatoes, peeled and sliced
1 aubergine/eggplant
120g/4oz mushrooms sliced
2 courgettes/zucchini
4 tomatoes, peeled and sliced
1 green pepper, sliced

TOMATO SAUCE
15ml/1 tbsp oil
1 onion, finely chopped
1 clove garlic, minced
1 400g/14oz can tomatoes
15ml/1 tbsp tomato purée/paste
1.25ml/¼ tsp ground cinnamon
1.25ml/¼ tsp ground cumin
Salt and pepper
Pinch of sugar

EGG SAUCE
30g/2 tbsps butter or margarine
30g/2 tbsps flour
280ml/½ pint/1 cup milk
1 egg, beaten
60g/2oz/½ cup feta cheese
Nutmeg
Salt and pepper

Cut the aubergine/eggplant in half and lightly score the cut surface. Sprinkle with salt and leave to stand for ½ hour. Put the potatoes into a roasting bag, seal and cook 10 minutes on HIGH. Heat the oil for the tomato sauce 30 seconds on HIGH. Add the onions and garlic and cook 1 minute on HIGH. Add the remaining ingredients and cook a further 6 minutes on HIGH. Wash the aubergine/eggplant well and dry. Slice it thinly and cook in 30ml/ 2 tbsps oil for 2 minutes on HIGH in a covered dish. Remove the slices and drain. Add the mushrooms to the dish and cook for 2 minutes on HIGH. Remove and set aside. Add the green pepper and the courgettes/ zucchini and cook for 1 minute on HIGH. Layer the vegetables, starting with the aubergine/eggplant and ending with the potatoes. Spoon the tomato sauce over each layer except the potatoes. Cook the butter for the egg sauce for 30 seconds on HIGH. Stir in the flour, nutmeg, salt and pepper. Add the milk gradually and cook for 3 minutes on HIGH, stirring after 1 minute. Add the cheese and egg and stir well to blend. Pour over the potatoes and cook 4 minutes on HIGH or 5 minutes on a combination setting in a microwave convection oven, or until set.

This page: Sweet and Sour Nuggets. Facing page: Vegetable Moussaka (top) and Mushrooms Florentine (bottom).

Sweet and Sour Nuggets

PREPARATION TIME: 25 minutes

MICROWAVE COOKING TIME: 15½-16½ minutes

SERVES: 4 people

60g/2oz/½ cup ground almonds
60g/2oz/½ cup finely chopped water chestnuts
30g/1oz/2 tbsps butter or margarine
1 shallot, finely chopped
30g/1oz/2 tbsps flour

5ml/1 tsp chopped parsley
5ml/1 tsp ground ginger
140ml/¼ pint/½ cup milk
1 beaten egg
Salt and pepper

COATING
Remaining beaten egg
Dry breadcrumbs
Sesame seeds
30-60ml/2-4 tbsps oil for frying

SWEET AND SOUR SAUCE
60g/2oz/¼ cup brown sugar
60ml/2 fl oz/¼ cup vinegar
30ml/2 tbsps tomato ketchup
30ml/2 tbsps soy sauce
1 225g/8oz can pineapple chunks/pieces
30g/2 tbsps cornstarch/cornflour
1 green pepper
2 green/spring onions, sliced
1 small can bamboo shoots

ACCOMPANIMENT
225g/8oz bean sprouts

Melt the butter for the nuggets for 1 minute on HIGH. Add the shallot and cook 30 seconds on HIGH. Stir in the flour and add the milk gradually. Cook for 2 minutes on HIGH until thickened. Add the remaining nugget ingredients and half the beaten egg. Spread the mixture into a square pan and chill until firm. Shape the mixture into an even number of 2.5cm/1 inch balls. Coat with the remaining egg and the dry breadcrumbs and sesame seeds, shaking off the excess. Heat a browning dish for 5 minutes on HIGH and pour in the oil. Put in the nuggets and cover the dish. Cook for 3-4 minutes on HIGH, turning frequently. Drain on paper towels. Combine the sugar, vinegar, ketchup, soy sauce, pineapple juice and cornstarch/cornflour in a small, deep bowl. Cook for 2-3 minutes on HIGH until thickened, stirring frequently. Add the peppers and onions and cook 1 minute on HIGH. Add the pineapple pieces and the bamboo shoots and cook a further 30 seconds on HIGH. Place the bean sprouts in a serving dish and heat 1 minute on HIGH. Put the nuggets in the middle. Coat over with the sweet and sour sauce to serve.

Japanese Steamer

PREPARATION TIME: 20 minutes
MICROWAVE COOKING TIME: 13 minutes
SERVES: 4 people

3 packages tofu, drained
16 dried black mushrooms, soaked and stems removed
120g/4oz small mushrooms
8 baby corn-on-the-cob
1 small diakon (mooli) radish, sliced
1 bunch fresh chives, left whole
120g/4oz buckwheat noodles or other variety Japanese noodles
1 package dried sea spinach
1 lemon, sliced

SAUCE
1 small piece fresh ginger root, grated
140ml/¼ pint/½ cup soy sauce
60ml/4 tbsps vegetable stock
15ml/1 tbsp sherry or white wine
5ml/1 tsp cornstarch/cornflour

Cover the noodles with 570ml/1 pint/2 cups water and a pinch of salt. Cook on HIGH for 6 minutes and leave to stand, covered, for 10 minutes before using. Put the mushrooms and spinach into 2 separate bowls, fill both bowls with water and leave the spinach to soak. Put the mushrooms into the microwave oven and heat for 5 minutes on HIGH and set aside. Put the small mushrooms and the baby corn-on-the-cob into a small bowl with 15ml/1 tbsp water. Cover the bowl with pierced cling film/plastic wrap and cook for 2 minutes on HIGH and set aside. Combine all the ingredients for the sauce in a glass measure. Cook on HIGH for 3 minutes or until thickened. Stir after 1 minute. Slice the tofu into 1.25cm/½ inch slices. Drain the black mushrooms and remove the stalks. Drain the noodles and arrange in 4 separate serving dishes. Add the spinach, tofu, whole black mushrooms and small mushrooms, baby ears of corn, radish slices, and lemon slices. Pour some of the sauce over each serving and garnish with the fresh chives. Heat the dishes through for 1 minute on HIGH and serve the remaining sauce separately.

Mushrooms Florentine

PREPARATION TIME: 20 minutes
MICROWAVE COOKING TIME: 17 minutes
SERVES: 4 people

60g/2oz/¼ cup butter or margarine
450g/1lb large mushrooms
900g/2lb fresh spinach, stalks removed and leaves washed
2 shallots, finely chopped
4 tomatoes, peeled, seeded and diced
Salt and pepper
Nutmeg

SAUCE
45g/3 tbsps butter or margarine
45g/3 tbsps flour
570ml/1 pint/2 cups milk
180g/6oz/1½ cups grated Cheddar cheese
2.5ml/½ tsp dry mustard
Pinch cayenne pepper
Salt and pepper
60g/2oz/¼ cup Parmesan cheese, grated
Paprika

Place the washed spinach in a large bowl or a roasting bag with a pinch of salt. Cover or seal and cook 4 minutes in the water that clings to the leaves. Set aside. Melt the butter in a large casserole for 30 seconds on HIGH. Cook the mushrooms for 3 minutes on HIGH, turning often. Remove the mushrooms and set them aside. Add the shallots to the butter in the bowl, cover, and cook 2 minutes on HIGH. Chop the spinach roughly and add to the shallots with the tomato, salt, pepper and nutmeg. Place in the bottom of the casserole dish and arrange the mushrooms on top. Melt the butter for the sauce 1 minute on HIGH. Stir in the flour, mustard, salt, pepper and a pinch of cayenne pepper. Add the milk gradually, beating until smooth. Cook, uncovered, 4 minutes on HIGH, stirring twice after 1 minute's cooking. Add Cheddar cheese and stir to melt. Coat over the mushrooms and spinach and sprinkle the Parmesan and paprika on top. Cook 3 minutes until bubbling.

Facing page: Japanese Steamer.

Escalopes d'Aubergines au Fromage

PREPARATION TIME: 25 minutes

MICROWAVE COOKING TIME: 14-15 minutes

SERVES: 4 people

1 large or 2 small aubergines/eggplants
Seasoned flour for coating
45ml/3 tbsps oil for frying

TOPPING
15g/1 tbsp butter
2 shallots, finely chopped
10ml/2 tsps chopped tarragon
10ml/2 tsps chopped chervil
225g/8oz cream cheese
120g/4oz/1 cup grated Gruyère or Swiss cheese
180ml/6 fl oz/¾ cup heavy/double cream
Dry breadcrumbs

VEGETABLES
12 small new potatoes
8 baby carrots
4 small turnips
4 small fresh beets
8 spring/green onions
4 very small courgettes/zucchini
120g/4oz French/green beans, trimmed
120g/4oz mangetout/peapods, trimmed
120g/4oz/½ cup butter, melted
Chopped parsley

Slice the aubergines/eggplants into 8 2.5cm/1 inch thick slices. Score the slices lightly on both sides and sprinkle with salt. Leave to stand for 30 minutes to draw out any bitterness. Melt the butter for the topping for 30 seconds on HIGH. Add the shallot and cook for 2 minutes. Cool and mix with the other topping ingredients, except the dry breadcrumbs, and set aside. Cook the vegetables in 60ml/2 fl oz/¼ cup salted water as follows:–
new potatoes for 10 minutes
baby carrots for 10 minutes
fresh beets for 8-9 minutes
turnips for 8 minutes
spring/green onion for 2-3 minutes
French/green beans for 2-3 minutes
courgettes/zucchini for 2-3 minutes
mangetout/peapods for 2-3 minutes.
Cook the vegetables in a loosely covered casserole and keep the beetroot separate. Melt the butter for 1 minute on HIGH and pour over the vegetables. Sprinkle the carrots and the new potatoes with chopped parsley. Leave the vegetables covered while preparing the aubergines/eggplants. Rinse the aubergines/eggplants well and pat dry. Mix the flour with salt and pepper and lightly coat the aubergine/eggplant slices. Heat a browning dish for 5 minutes on HIGH. Pour in the oil and put in the aubergine/eggplant slices. Cover the dish and cook for 2-3 minutes, turning halfway through the cooking time. Remove the aubergines/eggplants from the browning dish and drain them on paper towels. Place them in a clean casserole or on a plate and top each slice with a spoonful of the cheese mixture. Sprinkle on the dry breadcrumbs and

This page: Escalopes d'Aubergines au Fromage. Facing page: Pasta Spirals with Walnuts and Gorgonzola (top) and Forester's Pasta (bottom).

cook on MEDIUM for 2 minutes. Arrange on serving plates with the vegetables.

Macaroni, Cheese and Tomato Squares

PREPARATION TIME: 15 minutes

MICROWAVE COOKING TIME: 14 minutes plus 10 minutes standing time

SERVES: 4 people

225g/8oz/3 cups macaroni
60g/2oz/¼ cup butter or margarine

60g/2oz/4 tbsps flour
Pinch dry mustard
Pinch cayenne pepper
850ml/1½ pints/3 cups milk
120g/4oz/1 cup grated Cheddar cheese
Salt and pepper
2 tomatoes

Put the macaroni into a large bowl with 1150ml/2 pints/4 cups salted water. Cook on HIGH for 6 minutes and leave to stand, covered, for 10 minutes before draining. Melt the butter for 1 minute on HIGH and stir in the flour, mustard, cayenne pepper, salt and pepper. Add the milk gradually and cook for 3-4 minutes on HIGH, stirring after 1 minute. Add the cheese to the sauce and stir to melt. Drain the macaroni well and mix it with half of the sauce. Press the macaroni mixture into a 20cm/ 8 inch square pan and chill until firm. Dilute the remaining sauce with 280ml/½ pint/1 cup milk. When the macaroni mixture is firm, cut it into 8 squares and remove from the tin. Place on a serving dish and slice the tomatoes, putting 1 slice on top of each square. Reheat the sauce for 1 minute on HIGH and pour over the macaroni squares. Reheat the squares on a serving dish for 2 minutes on HIGH. Serve immediately.

Forester's Pasta

PREPARATION TIME: 15 minutes

MICROWAVE COOKING TIME: 18 minutes plus 10 minutes standing time

SERVES: 4 people

450g/1lb spinach and plain tagliatelle/ fettucine
2 carrots, shredded
90ml/3oz oyster or wild mushrooms
30g/2 tbsps butter or margarine
1 clove garlic
30ml/2 tbsps chopped herbs such as thyme, parsley and sage
180ml/½ pint/1 cup heavy/double cream
Salt and pepper
60g/2oz fresh Parmesan cheese, ungrated

Place the pasta in a large bowl with 1150ml/2 pints/4 cups hot water, a

pinch of salt and 15ml/1 tbsp oil. Cook for 6 minutes on HIGH. Cover and leave to stand 10 minutes before draining. Rinse in hot water and leave to dry. Heat a browning dish 5 minutes on HIGH. Melt the butter 1 minute and add the garlic and carrots. Cook 1 minute on HIGH. The garlic should brown slightly. Add the mushrooms and cook 1 minute further on HIGH. Add the herbs, cream, salt and pepper and cook 2 minutes on HIGH. Toss with the pasta. Use a cheese slicer or a knife to shave off thin slices of Parmesan cheese to serve on top.

Stuffed Vine Leaves

PREPARATION TIME: 25 minutes

MICROWAVE COOKING TIME: 26-34 minutes

SERVES: 4 people

1 package vine leaves

FILLING
180g/6oz/1½ cups rice
1 onion, finely chopped
60g/2 tbsps butter or margarine
120g/8oz/1 cup black olives, stoned and chopped
1 green pepper, chopped
120g/4oz/1 cup pine-nuts
120g/4oz/1 cup feta cheese, crumbled
30g/2 tbsps chopped parsley
5ml/1 tsp ground coriander

TOMATO SAUCE
1 400g/14oz can tomatoes
15ml/1 tbsp tomato purée/paste
1 onion, finely chopped
15ml/1 tbsp oil
1 clove garlic
1.25ml/¼ tsp cinnamon
1.25ml/¼ tsp ground cumin
Salt and pepper

If the vine leaves are packed in brine, soak them in cold water for 30 minutes before using. Cook the rice 8-10 minutes in 570ml/1 pint/2 cups water with a pinch of salt. Leave the rice to stand, covered, for 5 minutes. Melt the butter for 30 seconds on HIGH and add the onion, pepper and coriander. Cook for 2 minutes on HIGH. Stir in the drained rice,

cheese, parsley, salt and pepper. Fill the leaves and roll them up, tucking in the ends. Arrange the leaves in a baking dish and set aside while preparing the sauce. Heat the oil for the sauce 30 seconds on HIGH and add the onion and garlic and cook for 1 minute on HIGH. Add the remaining ingredients and cook 6 minutes on HIGH. Leave to stand for 5 minutes before pouring over the vine leaves. Cook the vine leaves for 16 minutes on HIGH. Garnish with more chopped parsley if desired.

Pasta Spirals with Walnuts and Gorgonzola

PREPARATION TIME: 15 minutes

MICROWAVE COOKING TIME: 12 minutes plus 10 minutes standing time

SERVES: 4 people

450g/1lb pasta spirals
450g/1lb Gorgonzola cheese
120g/4oz/1 cup walnut halves
280ml/½ pint/1 cup heavy/double cream
Coarsely ground pepper

GARNISH
2 ripe figs
4 sprigs fresh thyme

Place the pasta in a large bowl with 1150ml/2 pints/4 cups hot water, a pinch of salt and 15ml/1 tbsp oil. Cook for 6 minutes on HIGH. Cover and leave to stand for 10 minutes before draining. Rinse in hot water and leave to dry. Combine the cream and crumbled cheese in a deep bowl. Cook on MEDIUM for 4 minutes until the cheese melts. Do not stir too often. Add the walnut halves and the coarsely ground pepper. Taste, and add salt if desired. Pour over the pasta in a serving dish and toss to coat. Cut the figs in half and then in half again. Put one half fig on each plate with a sprig of thyme to garnish.

Facing page: Stuffed Vine Leaves (top) and Macaroni, Cheese and Tomato Squares (bottom).

DESSERTS

Avocado Creams

PREPARATION TIME: 25 minutes plus setting time

MICROWAVE COOKING TIME: 11½ minutes

SERVES: 4-6 people

2 eggs, separated
60g/2oz/4 tbsps sugar
430ml/¾ pint/1½ cups milk
2.5ml/½ tsp pistachio flavouring
15g/½ oz/1 tbsp gelatine or agar-agar
45ml/3 tbsps water and lemon juice mixed
1 large ripe avocado, well mashed
280g/½ pint/1 cup whipped cream

DECORATION
Pistachio nuts
Grated chocolate
Reserved whipped cream

Sprinkle the gelatine or agar-agar onto the liquid and leave it to soak. Beat the egg yolks and sugar together until thick and lemon coloured. Heat the milk for 5 minutes on HIGH until almost boiling. Gradually stir the milk into the eggs. Return to the microwave oven in a large glass measure. Heat for 6 minutes on LOW, whisking every 2 minutes until the mixture thickens. Have a bowl of iced water ready. Place the measure in the water to stop the cooking, and any time during cooking that the mixture seems about to curdle. Mash the avocado in a food processor until very smooth, combine with the custard and add the flavouring. Allow to cool. Melt the gelatine or agar-agar for 30 seconds on HIGH. Stir into the custard. Chill in the iced water until beginning to thicken, stirring constantly. Remove from the iced water while beating the egg whites until stiff but not dry. Fold into the custard with half of the whipped cream. Pour into the serving dish and chill until set. Decorate with the remaining cream piped into rosettes, pistachio nuts and grated chocolate.

Pumpkin Pecan Pudding

PREPARATION TIME: 15 minutes

MICROWAVE COOKING TIME: 19-23 minutes

SERVES: 4-6 people

60g/2oz/½ cup chopped pecans
30g/1oz/2 tbsps butter or margarine
225g/8oz/2 cups canned pumpkin
2.5ml/1 tsp ground cinnamon
2.5ml/½ tsp ground ginger
Pinch ground cloves
Pinch nutmeg
90g/3oz/⅓ cup cream cheese
90ml/3 fl oz/⅓ cup evaporated milk
3 eggs
120g/4oz/½ cup sugar

DECORATION
140ml/¼ pint/½ cup whipped cream
Preserved/crystallised ginger, sliced
Angelica, cut in thin strips

Heat the butter for 30 seconds on HIGH. Stir in the pecans and cook a further 1 minute on HIGH. In a deep bowl, beat the remaining ingredients together until smooth. Add the buttered pecans. Cook on HIGH for 3 minutes, stirring halfway through. Reduce the setting to MEDIUM and cook 15-20 minutes or until thickened. Pour into a large serving dish or individual ramekins/custard cups. Leave to stand at least 15 minutes before serving, or chill and decorate with piped cream and slices of ginger and angelica.

Halva of Carrots and Cashews

PREPARATION TIME: 15 minutes

MICROWAVE COOKING TIME: 20 minutes

SERVES: 4-6 people

1kg/2lbs carrots, peeled and shredded
280ml/½ pint/1 cup heavy/double cream
180g/6oz/¾ cup dark brown sugar
30ml/2 tbsps honey
60g/2oz/¼ cup raisins
60g/2oz/¼ cup butter or margarine
10ml/2 tsps ground coriander
5ml/1 tsp ground cinnamon
Pinch saffron
120g/4oz/1 cup chopped, unsalted, roasted cashews

DECORATION
Candied violets
Silver leaf or silver argentées/balls
Desiccated coconut

Cook the carrots, milk, sugar, honey and spices in a large bowl for 15 minutes on HIGH. Cook uncovered. Add the butter, raisins, nuts and cook for 5 minutes on HIGH, stirring frequently until thick. It may be necessary to add 2-3 more minutes cooking time to thicken. Allow the mixture to cool and pile onto serving dishes. Decorate with violets, silver leaf or argentées/balls and coconut. Serve warm or chilled with cream if desired.

Facing page: Halva of Carrots and Cashews (top), Avocado Creams (center) and Pumpkin Pecan Pudding (bottom).

Microwave

VEGETARIAN

INDEX